KEEP SMILING THROUGH

Lisa Evans

KEEP SMILING THROUGH

OBERON BOOKS
LONDON

WWW.OBERONBOOKS.COM

First published in 2011 by Oberon Books Ltd

521 Caledonian Road, London N7 9RH

Tel: +44 (0) 20 7607 3637 / Fax: +44 (0) 20 7607 3629

e-mail: info@oberonbooks.com

www.oberonbooks.com

A catalogue record for this book is available from the British Library.

ISBN: 978-1-84943-014-2

Cover image by John Swannell

Cover design Infinite Design

To Jenny

Keep Smiling Through was first presented at Theatre by the Lake, Keswick on Saturday 30 July 2011.

Cast list:

PERCE	Matt Addis
ROB	Benjamin Askew
HILDA	Fiona Drummond
ALEC	Ben Ingles
GRAN	Kate Layden
PEG	Polly Lister
JEAN	Olivia Mace
LEONORE	Heather Phoenix
MAGGIE	Heather Saunders

Production credits:
Director: Ian Forrest
Assistant Director: Jez Pike
Designer: Martin Johns
Musical Director/Arranger: Richard Atkinson
Assistant Musical Director: Kieran Buckeridge
Movement Director: Lorelei Lynn
Dialect Coach: Charmian Hoare
Fight Director: Peter Macqueen
Lighting Designer: Nick Beadle
Sound Designer: Andrew J Lindsay

Characters

MAGGIE
Keswick housewife in her 20s

PEG
Her best friend and sister-in-law, 20s

GRAN
Maggie's confused grandmother, 60s

HILDA
13-year-old Geordie evacuee billetted
with Maggie

LEONORE
German refugee, 40

JEAN
Landgirl and Maggie's lodger, 20

PERCE
Peg's older brother, farmhand, mid 30s

ALEC
Locum doctor, 30s

ROB
Maggie's husband, and Peg and Perce's
brother, RAF, 20s

EVACUEES
4 children aged 12-14. Non-speaking

The action takes place in Keswick
in autumn/winter 1940
in Maggie's kitchen, a church hall and the
Pavilion theatre front and backstage.

Act One

Opening song: "Sing As We Go"

SCENE 1

Church hall, Keswick. Mid-November. Lunchtime.

PERCE and DR ALEC are manhandling an upright piano into the hall filled with bags of clothes, folding tables, cardboard boxes etc full of assorted collections, a rail of clothes can partition space and be moved where most inconvenient as characters try to defend their personal space/ work area. A small gang of four evacuee children under 14 ineffectually help, get in the way as MAGGIE tries to shoo them away.

PERCE: *(Off.)* You over the top, Doctor?

ALEC: Nearly. Slightly to the left. Mind the door jamb… Ow!

> *He catches his hand. MAGGIE hurries over from where she's been attending to GRAN, sat in a corner with some unravelling.*

MAGGIE: Stay put Gran. I'll be right back. Hilda.

> *Answering MAGGIE's gesture, HILDA, a quiet watchful child, helps GRAN.*

PERCE: *(Off.)* What? No, you're not helping.

MAGGIE: Out of the way, you lot. You all right?

ALEC: *(Smiling through the pain.)* Fine. I've got another one.

PERCE: *(Off.)* Sorry?

MAGGIE: He's hurt his hand Perce! *(She leans over the piano.)* Perce the doctor's hurt his hand.

PERCE: *(Off.)* Hurt what?

ALEC: No, I'm all right really. Big shove now Perce and then she'll roll I think.

PERCE: *(Off.)* Yan, tan, tethera, push!

The piano moves on castors into the room followed by PERCE, PEG and LEONORE, all hot and sweaty.

PEG: Blimey, you better not change your mind Maggie. I'm not pushing that back up to your place.

MAGGIE: As if I would. I'm glad to be shot of it.

ALEC: Where do you want it?

MAGGIE: Oh out of the way somewhere. What d'you think Leonore, you're the one going to be using it most?

PEG: What about in that corner?

MAGGIE: She'll freeze there. There's fine.

PEG: We'll all freeze if that stove doesn't get a bit of a move on.

ALEC and PERCE push the piano into a corner.

MAGGIE: The wood's damp.

PEG: Everything's damp this time of year.

Once they've got it set up, LEONORE sits down and does a few scales and then plays.

MAGGIE: Hilda love, see if the kettle's boiled and if it has make a brew. Remember, take the

PEG: *(Joining in.)* Pot to the kettle, not the kettle to the pot.

HILDA: I know.

HILDA moves off. PEG and MAGGIE start to sort the bags of clothing. During their next interchange PERCE gets a free consultation with DR ALEC.

PEG: She's all right really. For a Geordie. At least you can understand what she's saying.

MAGGIE: Oh she's no trouble.

PEG: That's right, rub it in.

MAGGIE: Sidney's…

PEG: Sidney's nothing but.

MAGGIE: He's got an enquiring mind.

PEG: He's got the devil in him. I wonder if he has German blood somewhere.

MAGGIE: *(Looking towards LEONORE.)* Ssh.

PEG: Now if I was religious I'd say "Know thine enemy".

MAGGIE: But Peg, you're not.

PEG: What?

MAGGIE: Religious. Only time you've been inside a church in the past 15 years aside from Christmas and Easter Sunday was last June.

PEG: You can't get married in registry office!

MAGGIE: Plenty do.

PEG: Anyway there was Sunday school.

MAGGIE: We only went for three weeks and that was for the crayons.

PEG: So? I can have an opinion. Keswick's still a free country.

MAGGIE: *(Laughing.)* What?

PEG: You know what I mean.

MAGGIE: It can't be easy, being a foreigner.

PEG: *(Nodding to the kids.)* This lot seem to manage.

MAGGIE: Hey leave that stuff alone. Go on. Off with you. Go and do something useful.

The kids leave.

We collected five pounds of hips at the weekend. That'll fetch a few bob. How about you?

PEG: Don't recall.

MAGGIE: You must do.

PEG: They're not going to cheat us. It's war effort. Everything's war effort.

HILDA brings tea for the men and LEONORE.

MAGGIE: What's up with you?

PEG: It's just dull. We're like old women, spending our days sorting bags of other people's cast offs. When my mum was just married my dad was home every night. Instead I've got Alf away getting up to God knows what…

MAGGIE: Alf wouldn't.

PEG: I've not heard from him in a fortnight.

MAGGIE: He's probably just lost somewhere.

PEG: And that's supposed to make me feel better? They could shoot him Maggie. Leastways when he was home taxiing, worst that could happen was the fare refused to pay. How he passed out of Portinscale I'll never know. What if he drives across enemy lines or something?

MAGGIE: They don't have them in Cumberland. Anyway I doubt they'll let him navigate. Not with his history. He probably just drives his truck where he's told.

PEG: He'd be good at that. His mum always says he was born with a steering wheel in his hands, which must have been the other side of painful at the time.

MAGGIE: Better than Charlie Pepper.

PEG: How d'you mean?

MAGGIE: You know what Lorna's always saying. "My Charlie was born playing the violin."

PEG: No wonder she's bow legged. "My Charlie is always top of the class."

MAGGIE: "My Charlie's in the RAF you know."

PEG: Oh I could tell Lorna Pepper a thing or two about her darling son. Yesterday when she was telling us how to organise our stall I was so tempted. Remember when we were 16, he paid us to kiss him in Hope Park?

MAGGIE: Paid you.

PEG: Yeah. Good money too. Thing was, daft bugger, I'd a done it for free.

MAGGIE: What d'you mean "would've"? You did, on a regular basis if memory serves.

PEG: Yeah.

MAGGIE: My summer as a gooseberry.

PEG: No time for regrets now.

MAGGIE: Indeed. You being a newly married woman and all.

PEG: Charlie was just a you know, growing up thing. But he was always a nice looking lad.

MAGGIE: Except for the taxi door ears.

PEG: If he'd been my kid I'd have stuck them to his head at birth.

MAGGIE: Maybe the flying helmets'll help.

PEG: You heard from Rob lately?

MAGGIE: Yeah, he's got leave in a fortnight. All being well.

PEG: Leave! Oh Maggie, why didn't you say?!

MAGGIE: Didn't want to count my chickens.

PEG: Our Rob home!

MAGGIE: I know.

PEG: You've got that look.

MAGGIE: No I haven't.

PEG: You have. Like that time you first confessed you were sweet on him.

MAGGIE: Get off.

PEG: Yeah. All lit up like you got Christmas inside. What? What've I said? Oh, don't take on.

MAGGIE: *(Wiping her eyes.)* I just want him home safe so bad.

PEG: Course you do.

MAGGIE: But I'm frightened if I talk about it I'll jinx him somehow. I've even found myself praying, to a God I don't believe in, and if I did, why would he think my husband's safety more important than anyone else's?

PEG: Because you and Rob were made for each other. Keswick's answer to Romeo and Juliet.

MAGGIE: Peg. They both died.

PEG: Ah. What're you going to wear?

MAGGIE: I don't know.

PEG: You got to make an effort.

MAGGIE: I thought the yellow print maybe.

PEG: You'll freeze.

MAGGIE: I'll wear my vest, and a cardie.

PEG: Really romantic.

MAGGIE: I don't do romance.

PEG: Rubbish. Can't let yourself go you know.

MAGGIE: I'm busy.

PEG: And our Rob looks so smart in his uniform.

MAGGIE: Yes, he does. *(Loyally.)* So does Alf.

PEG: Alf couldn't look smart if you dipped him in starch! Soppy aporth. Hey you and me should go out.

MAGGIE: Why?

PEG: Like we used to.

MAGGIE: We've no husbands.

PEG: There's plenty of men.

MAGGIE: Peg!

PEG: Just to dance with. Oh go on. There's a tea dance Saturday at the Pavilion.

MAGGIE: I know.

PEG: How?

MAGGIE: I'm doing the refreshments.

PEG: That's settled then. What'll we wear?

MAGGIE: Yellow print I expect. Doesn't matter, I'll have a pinny on.

PEG: Maggie.

MAGGIE: Leonore said she'd put a frill on that'd make all the difference.

PEG: What does she know about fashion?

MAGGIE: It's what she used to do before the war, back home.

PEG: In Germany? I'll make do with what I've got.

MAGGIE: I'm sure she'd help you if you asked.

PEG: Thanks but no.

MAGGIE: She'll miss coming round ours now her piano lessons will be here. I don't imagine Lorna's exactly great company of an evening. In fact I know she's not. She makes Leonore have her tea alone in the kitchen.

PEG: I'll manage.

MAGGIE spots the doctor leaving.

MAGGIE: Oh are you off?

ALEC: Better make a move. Rounds to do.

PEG: Is it true the locum doctor always gets the difficult patients?

ALEC: I'll let you know when I've been here a bit longer.

MAGGIE: You never got your tea!

ALEC: Yes I did, Hilda gave me a cup.

MAGGIE: What about a bun? Freshly baked yesterday? We're starting doing teas for the drivers.

ALEC: No I'm fine.

MAGGIE: I must, after all your help.

ALEC: Really. My pleasure. Cheerio. Perce.

PERCE: Bye doctor. And you think I shouldn't worry about…?

ALEC: Keep it clean and put a plaster on it.

ALEC leaves crossing with JEAN who manages to look good even in her landgirl uniform.

PEG: *(Disapproving.)* Alec?

ALEC: Sorry Jean, just off.

JEAN: Alec! How lovely to see you.

MAGGIE shrugs.

MAGGIE: That's Jean.

JEAN: Off to minister to the sick and needy? Rather you than me. Though I did flirt with the idea of the nurse's uniform. So much better than this.

ALEC: Cap and apron wouldn't keep you very warm up on the fells.

JEAN: Yes. Probably better to wear the dress as well. I've made you blush. I'm sorry. I didn't think one could embarrass doctors.

PEG: *(Giggling to MAGGIE.)* Did she really just say that?

ALEC: They try and train it out of you but…in my case…not very effectively.

He makes to leave.

MAGGIE: Thanks so much for your help.

ALEC: Cheerio.

JEAN: Bye then! Hello everyone. Just popped in to see how the grand piano move had gone.

LEONORE exits to the kitchen.

PEG: It's an upright.

JEAN: *(Laughing.)* Too funny. I have had the most awful day you could ever imagine. How people run up and down those hills

PEG/MAGGIE: Fells.

JEAN: Whichever, how they do that for pleasure is totally beyond me. As for sheep, no wonder they all end up as jumpers or mutton. They absolutely deserve it. Stupidest creatures I've ever met, apart from the Bradbury sisters.

PEG: Who were the Bradbury sisters?

JEAN: Girls at school. Thick as planks.

PEG: What did they end up as?

JEAN: Who knows, something in Whitehall I expect. Daddy was a Viscount. Gosh I'm tired.

PEG nudges MAGGIE to look at PERCE who has stood, mouth open, staring at JEAN since she entered.

Can I come and sit with you for a minute Mrs S to get warm?

GRAN: Hello dear.

JEAN: I must look an absolute sight. The wind out there today. Is my hair standing on end?

GRAN: Yes.

JEAN: Oh you are such a character. You should meet my grandmother. She's mean as hell. Reeks of Chanel, gin and mothballs.

PEG: Perce. You're catching flies.

PERCE: What?

PEG: How did I end up with two such different brothers? Bet you're glad you got Rob instead of this one.

PEG pushes his jaw shut.

GRAN: Do I know you?

JEAN: Oh dear, one of those days? I'm the one in the back bedroom. Gasper?

GRAN: Can I have a cup of tea?

HILDA heads off to get it.

MAGGIE: She's getting worse. She went out back to feed the chickens this morning, found her half an hour later at the bus stop chatting with Loudey Pete.

PEG: She'd be safe with him.

MAGGIE: Chicken she had under her arm wouldn't.

PEG: Be better now you've not got all the rodent girls traipsing in and out for their piano lessons.

MAGGIE: Just have them here instead.

PEG: Not the same as having your home invaded though is it? Mind, I'd not say no to a landgirl if she was as nice as Jean. But it wouldn't be fair.

MAGGIE: With Sidney you mean?

PEG: I was thinking of Perce. But Sidney too, you're right.

MAGGIE: And Peg, could you resist calling the Rodean girls rodents, at least while they're in hearing distance?

PEG: Rodents, Brown Bombers, they've all got nicknames.

She holds up a smart frock.

Here, this is nice.

MAGGIE: Should fetch a bob or two next sale.

PEG: No one'd notice.

MAGGIE: Folks aren't donating their possessions to see the likes of you and me dressing up as ladies.

PEG: I'm working for nothing. Should be some perks. Original owners didn't graft to get them, I bet. Perce?

PERCE: What?

PEG: Haven't you got work to be getting on with?

PERCE: What?

PEG: The rabbit run?

MAGGIE: You've got rabbits? Since when?

PEG: Yesterday.

MAGGIE: Oh.

PEG: Well you've chickens.

HILDA brings tea for GRAN. LEONORE sits back at the piano.

MAGGIE: All the same.

PEG: Face it love, no point competing with me. Thought you'd learned that years ago.

MAGGIE: Shut up.

PERCE: Would you like to see my rabbits?

JEAN: What? Oh absolutely.

PERCE: They're very soft.

JEAN: Do they bite? Can't abide creatures that bite.

MAGGIE: Bit of a handicap as a landgirl isn't it?

JEAN: There's always crops. I'm absolutely wizard with those. Hay, corn, hay, that sort of thing.

HILDA: Could I see the rabbits? Please?

MAGGIE: Go on Perce, take her. Then off to school, right? And don't forget the bag of hips on your way. 5lbs we picked over the weekend. How many did Sidney get?

PEG: I don't know how many he picked, but he lost most of them.

MAGGIE: Lost them, how?

PEG: In a game, he said. Ammo apparently.

HILDA: Sidney's always the Nazis.

PEG: Is he now? There's a surprise.

HILDA: And everyone else is the Allies.

MAGGIE: If only.

PERCE leaves with HILDA, reluctantly.

HILDA: Do the rabbits have names?

PERCE: Aye. Stew.

JEAN: Stewart. How sweet. *(She laughs.)* Oh isn't this just bliss. I like it things being all shaken up, don't you?

LEONORE starts to play"Lili Marlene".

MAGGIE: Not really. Mostly I like to know where things are.

PEG: She's a home bird is our Maggie. Known for it.

JEAN: Just think, if it wasn't for the Jerries we'd never have met. They can't be all bad. Or maybe they can. If only people didn't get killed war would be such fun.

PEG: How about something a bit more patriotic? As in not German.

MAGGIE: Peg.

PEG: I'm just saying. If we're going to win the war…

GRAN: *Singing: "We Must All Stick Together"*

JEAN: Oh gosh what've I started?

MAGGIE: *(Laughing.)* Gran.

GRAN continues undaunted. When singing she has perfect recall.

MAGGIE: It's no good. She's off.

GRAN: *Singing*

PEG joins in, JEAN hums along. GRAN waves her teacup like a beer mug.

PEG: Come on Maggie. No one can hear us.

MAGGIE shrugs and joins in.

JEAN starts to dance around, PEG joins her in improv routine.

ALL: Chorus

End of scene.

Scene change song: "We Must All Stick Together"

SCENE 2

MAGGIE's kitchen. Five days later, early Saturday evening.

HILDA is sitting close to the range unravelling a jumper. A large ball of mud-coloured wool rolls onto the stage followed slowly by GRAN who is knitting a portion of a tank camouflage net on very large needles. She knits her way towards the ball of wool. HILDA picks up the ball and winds it, moving towards gran. When they meet HILDA tucks the ball of wool into GRAN's apron pocket. GRAN looks at her puzzled for a moment.

HILDA: *(Reminding her.)* Hilda?

GRAN: Where did you spring from?

HILDA: Newcastle on Tyne

GRAN kisses HILDA on the forehead.

GRAN: *(Consoling.)* Never mind.

They both sit in the corner by the range, one knitting, one unravelling. JEAN, MAGGIE and PEG enter. They are preparing to go out for the tea dance.

PEG: So what do you think Jean? I could do her a few curls round the front and then roll the back up like so?

MAGGIE swats her away.

MAGGIE: I don't need anything doing. I'm fine as I am.

JEAN: Curls here and here I think. Modom will look ravishing for her evening behind the tea urn.

MAGGIE: Exactly. Who's going to be looking at me anyway?

PEG: So, if someone was looking you'd be interested?

MAGGIE: That's not what I meant and you know it.

PEG: Sit. Come on. It'll be fun to have a new look. I'll do mine too.

MAGGIE: Terrific. We can both look like trollops.

JEAN is mixing gravy browning with water from the kettle. The front of her hair is curly.

JEAN: Thanks very much.

MAGGIE: I didn't mean…

PEG: We'll look like sisters. Let's pretend we're sisters.

JEAN: Why?

PEG: That's what we used to do, didn't we Maggie?

JEAN: *(Painting her legs brown.)* How old were you?

MAGGIE: *(Dead pan.)* Twenty-one.

JEAN looks amazed.

PEG: *(Combing setting lotion into MAGGIE's hair and putting in curls secured by kirby grips.)* We were still at school so around thirteen I suppose.

JEAN: Didn't everyone here know you weren't?

PEG: Oh yes. It were just for fun.

Beat.

Didn't you ever do that sort of thing?

JEAN: Yes, only with ponies.

MAGGIE starts to giggle, PEG elbows her. They try not to laugh.

JEAN: For about a year I actually thought I was a horse.

JEAN does a horse impression, tossing her mane and whinnying.

MAGGIE: What made you stop?

JEAN: One of them bit me. Vicious little Shetland called Pinkie. He had remarkably large teeth for someone only this high.

She gestures to her buttock.

I've still got the scar. D'you want to… [see]?

MAGGIE: *(Before she can show them.)* We believe you!

JEAN: After that I entered my religious phase, thought I had the calling, that sort of thing. Mummy threatened to have me locked up, till it was pointed out that was sort of what happened in a convent anyway.

PEG: *(To MAGGIE, her mouth full of grips.)* Stay still or I'll have your eye out.

MAGGIE: You nearly done?

PEG: Mmm hmm.

MAGGIE: You've got a trickle just above your ankle.

JEAN: How's that?

PEG: Just the ticket.

MAGGIE: Ow!

PEG: You've got to bear pain to be beautiful.

MAGGIE: As I'll never be that I don't see the point. Hilda love can you give the chicken's mash a stir for us?

HILDA does as she's asked.

PEG: There you go.

JEAN: Me next. Can you do my seams now?

PEG: They won't be dry yet.

JEAN: I'll risk it.

JEAN gets up on a chair.

PEG: When am I getting ready?

MAGGIE: I'll do it.

PEG looks in a hand mirror.

PEG: God I look that washed out.

JEAN: Spot of lipstick on your cheeks'll do the trick. Come here.

JEAN turns to apply the lipstick.

MAGGIE: Now you've wriggled.

MAGGIE holds a corner of her apron up to JEAN's mouth.

MAGGIE: Spit.

JEAN: I'm sorry?

MAGGIE: Spit. On here.

JEAN: Me?

MAGGIE: Well I can't do it, we're not related.

JEAN spits and MAGGIE wipes off the wriggly line on JEAN's leg.

How far up do you want it?

JEAN: Oh all the way I think, don't you?

MAGGIE: Jean!

PEG giggles.

JEAN: Don't pretend you're shocked. I know you're not really. You're an old married lady.

MAGGIE: But you're not.

PEG: And less of the old. I'm only four months younger than her.

MAGGIE: You've got to be careful, Jean.

JEAN: Oh I am, I've told you. And I wouldn't lie to you Maggie, ever. It's just it's so hard when you're in love and it could be the last time you see him.

MAGGIE: See who? Who are we talking about this time?

JEAN: Mike of course.

MAGGIE: No of course about it. If I recall it were Davey a fortnight ago, then before him there was that airman in October.

JEAN: Julian. He was lovely.

PEG: I take it back. I do feel old.

JEAN: That's just because you're under the weather. An evening's dancing and you'll be right as rain.

MAGGIE: I didn't know you weren't well. You didn't say?

PEG: Oh it's nothing.

MAGGIE: What sort of nothing?

PEG: I'm fine now. There is that better?

She has two bright spots on her cheeks and lipstick on her lips.

JEAN: Peachy.

PEG: Maybe you should draw the stocking tops on as well while you're at it.

JEAN: And suspenders. What a hoot!

MAGGIE: I'm not that good at drawing.

PEG grabs the pencil.

PEG: I am. Give it here. Put your foot up on the table. That's it.

MAGGIE moves things out of the way.

JEAN: No tickling.

PEG: Remember who you're talking to. Keep still.

MAGGIE: Oh Hilda, there's a letter from your mum. I put it here to show you and forgot. I am sorry.

HILDA: Thank you Aunty Maggie.

HILDA starts for the door.

MAGGIE: You don't have to go upstairs you know. You could read it here in the warm if you wanted.

HILDA: It's okay, thank you.

HILDA leaves.

MAGGIE: She'll sit up there in that cold bedroom now reading that letter over and over for hours.

PEG: Sidney's family never write. I bet they're glad to be shot of him.

JEAN: He'll settle in soon.

PEG: Oh he's very relaxed. It's the rest of us who're about to evacuate. Somebody, who shall be nameless, gave him his old pea shooter and now our Rex's gone off his food and taken to sleeping in the coal shed. If it does come on to snow and he freezes solid I shall hold Sidney Melman personally responsible. There you go. How's that for a suspender?

JEAN and MAGGIE look.

MAGGIE: Very nice.

JEAN: It' s a bit...well big, isn't it?

GRAN wanders over to have a look.

MAGGIE: Can I get you something Gran?

GRAN: You could get me one of those. Is she joining the Navy?

PEG: It's not a tattoo.

GRAN: I'd still like one. Reminds me of my Arthur on our wedding night.

GRAN knits her way back to her chair.

PEG: Oh my God. I swear I didn't mean to draw that!

MAGGIE: I was wondering.

PEG: It's a suspender I promise.

JEAN: A very well developed one.

MAGGIE: (*Holding up the corner of her apron.*)

Spit.

JEAN spits and MAGGIE scrubs at her leg.

I'd stick to hairdressing Peg, if you don't want to end up arrested.

PEG: I drew a suspender! How many times!

MAGGIE: Yeah, yeah, and Sidney's the angel Gabriel.

They are all laughing so much they haven't heard PERCE enter.

PEG: Perce!

PERCE stands open mouthed. JEAN pulls her skirt down.

JEAN: Hello! We were just getting ready to go out.

PERCE: It's snowing.

MAGGIE: I can see, all over my floor. Haven't you heard of knocking?

PERCE: I did. But nobody came.

PEG: What's he done now?

PERCE: Who?

PEG: Sidney of course. What's he broken?

PERCE: Nothing. I've taken the matches off him.

PEG: Dear God…

MAGGIE: So what do you want, Perce?

PERCE: (*To JEAN.*) I brought you this.

He takes a dead rabbit out of his pocket. JEAN shrieks and steps back.

PERCE: It's all right. It won't bite.

PEG: Ain't that the truth.

MAGGIE: It'll have trouble doing anything now.

PERCE: It's for you.

PERCE hands the rabbit to JEAN who looks as if she's about to be sick.

JEAN: Maggie?

MAGGIE takes the rabbit.

MAGGIE: Thanks Perce. We'll have a nice pie for Sunday lunch. Make a change from fatherless stew. And maybe a fur collar for your winter coat Jean?

JEAN: Thanks. So much. I'll just go and…get ready…upstairs.

PEG: Try some lipstick on your cheeks.

JEAN exits hurriedly.

I thought the gentry spent their entire time hunting and killing wild creatures.

MAGGIE: I don't think she's that sort of gentry. Or if she was, I doubt she fitted in very well.

PEG: *(To PERCE.)* I wouldn't wait around. We're off out.

PERCE hesitates.

Was there something else?

PERCE: Message. From Lorna Pepper. Pass the word around there's to be a concert party in aid of Wings for Victory with prizes at the end with a judge from off the wireless.

PEG: Not Mr Walpole?

MAGGIE: He'd have a job. He died. Last summer.

PEG: Did he? No one told me.

MAGGIE: It was in the Reminder.

PERCE: So it must be true.

MAGGIE: Who's the entertainment?

PERCE: Us. We are. Anybody that wants. If they're good enough.

PEG: What d'you mean, good enough? Who decides?

PERCE: I don't know.

MAGGIE: Probably Lorna Pepper.

PERCE: They don't want just any old riff-raff.

PEG: Definitely Lorna Pepper.

PERCE: I thought I might do my bird impressions.

MAGGIE: Why not?

PERCE: Aye.

Beat.

PEG: She's not coming down again till we go out.

PERCE: Aye. Best go and have a practice.

MAGGIE: Good idea.

PERCE leaves.

PEG: Why are you encouraging him?

MAGGIE: He might meet somebody. You never know. Somebody nice.

PEG: Somebody more his type you mean?

MAGGIE: Well, honestly. Did you see her face when he pulled Benjamin Bunny out of his coat?

PEG: It's no good. You know how he gets, once he's a bee in his bonnet.

MAGGIE: So?

PEG: Nothing. He'll just have to get his heart broken I suppose. Could you do my legs now?

PEG holds out the pencil.

MAGGIE: I meant, so, what about you?

PEG: I'll get up here, shall I?

MAGGIE: Margaret Mary Maureen McKenzie. How long have we known each other?

PEG: Since the Christmas I was the Virgin Mary, Charlie Pepper tied my plaits to the donkey and you brained him with your crook.

MAGGIE: And who do we tell everything to first?

PEG: I told you I was going to marry Alf before he had any idea of my answer.

MAGGIE: That was because you hadn't asked him yet.

PEG: If I'd have waited for him I'd be an old maid now.

MAGGIE: So?

PEG: So, I haven't told anybody and… Yes.

MAGGIE beams.

I am.

And hugs her.

You don't mind?

MAGGIE: Why should I?

PEG: Well it's happened so quick for me.

MAGGIE: I'd mind if you told someone else first. It's wonderful.

PEG: Isn't it though? Just think Maggie, you'll be an aunty. A real one. Not like with Hilda. Oh come on, hurry up with those legs, I want to dance till I drop! We'll stop at Postlethwaite's on the way for chips. Celebrate. Can I borrow your pink scarf, don't want the snow ruining my hair?

MAGGIE: You know where to find it. Help yourself.

MAGGIE clears up the gravy browning, gives the mash on the stove a last stir and takes the pins out of her hair. Shrieks offstage from JEAN and PEG laughing as they get ready. MAGGIE goes over to GRAN.

MAGGIE: Gran we're off out for a couple of hours. It's snowing so you'd be best off stopping here by the fire. Hilda's upstairs and I'll put the wireless on for you. ITMAR'll be on soon. You like Tommy Handley.

GRAN: Do I?

MAGGIE turns on the radio. Dance music plays softly.

MAGGIE: Knitting's coming along well.

GRAN: Oddest sock I've ever seen.

MAGGIE: That's cos it's for a tank.

GRAN: What will they think of next?

MAGGIE: Camouflage netting. So it can't be spotted from the air.

GRAN: It's all beyond me.

HILDA enters quietly, her letter in her hand, and watches in the shadows.

MAGGIE: Never mind, you're doing your bit.

GRAN: Maggie?

MAGGIE: Yes Gran. That's me.

GRAN: I waited two miscarriages and four years till I fell for your mother. When the influenza took her I tried to catch it too.

MAGGIE: I know. But it was a long time ago now.

GRAN: Clear as day to me.

MAGGIE: Memory's funny like that.

GRAN: And there was you, looking just like her at that age, all long legs and wild hair, dragging me back. Gran do this, Gran do that.

MAGGIE: Gave you the runaround, did I?

GRAN: Your child…

MAGGIE: Yes?

GRAN: Your child will come.

MAGGIE: I know. We'll see.

PEG and JEAN enter all dolled up.

PEG: How do we look?

JEAN: Like a couple of starlets from Hollywood?

MAGGIE: Don't tempt me!

PEG: You haven't even got your pinny off. Jean, lipstick.

MAGGIE: I don't need it.

JEAN: Course you do.

LEONORE: *(Off.)* Hello? Please? Can I come in?

LEONORE enters as PEG is whisking off MAGGIE's pinny, fluffing up her hair, putting on her coat, while JEAN applies lipstick and powder.

JEAN: Hello Leonore. Is it still snowing?

LEONORE: Yes, very heavily. Like blankets.

JEAN: Are you going to play for the concert party?

LEONORE: I'm afraid yes. Mrs Lorna Pepper is determined.

PEG: Nothing new there! There you are Maggie, all set to go.

MAGGIE: Did you want something particular?

LEONORE: Mrs Pepper asked me to give you a telephone message.

MAGGIE: She sent you all the way up here in this weather? I'm manning the tea urn with her in twenty minutes!

Beat.

What's happened?

PEG: Is it Rob?

LEONORE: Yes, but it is good news. In five days' time he's coming home on leave.

PEG lets out a shriek of delight. MAGGIE smiles with relief. PEG swirls her round.

PEG: Switch on the lights!

MAGGIE laughs.

He's coming home! Rob's coming home!

JEAN: Hurrah!

JEAN turns up the volume on the wireless and to the sounds of GRAN singing along to "There's A Boy Coming Home On Leave" she and PEG whirl MAGGIE into a dance. LEONORE leaves.

End of scene

Scene change song: "There's A Boy Coming Home On Leave"

SCENE THREE

MAGGIE's kitchen. Three days later, Tuesday afternoon.

GRAN is sitting at the table, her head under a towel, inhaling.

GRAN: Help! Help!

MAGGIE is hanging up hanks of wool on the airer over the stove.

MAGGIE: Gran, just breathe.

GRAN: I can't! The lights have gone out.

MAGGIE: Yeah, I know, all over Europe.

GRAN: Maggie? Help! Help me!

MAGGIE: You breathe in the dark every night without help.

MAGGIE peeks in under the towel.

GRAN: Oh hello. Is it morning?

MAGGIE: Nearly teatime, and you've got a bad chest.

GRAN: I'm not surprised, spending all night under a damp towel.

MAGGIE: Ten minutes actually. All right. Out you come then. Steam's gone now anyway.

GRAN: *(Coughing.)* I'm not well.

MAGGIE: I know Gran. That's why the kitchen reeks of Friar's Balsam. Let's get you settled by the stove. Hilda will be home soon for her tea. And Jean off out gallivanting I've no doubt. You get a bit of shut eye while you can.

MAGGIE tucks GRAN up in her chair in a bundle of shawls.

MAGGIE: There you go. Snug as a bug in a rug. Sleepy?

GRAN grunts, already beginning to drift off. MAGGIE puts on the wireless low volume. She clears up the inhaling jug, hangs the towel over the range, picks up her knitting of a tiny baby matinee jacket and sitting, sings along softly with "You Must Have Been A Beautiful Baby". She jumps when ALEC enters.

ALEC: Sorry, I did knock but not very loudly. Just in case your Gran was resting.

MAGGIE: She's sleeping a lot at the minute.

ALEC: That's good.

MAGGIE: Is it?

ALEC: Yes.

MAGGIE: You sure?

ALEC: Trust me. I'm a doctor.

MAGGIE: Sorry. I didn't mean… Would you like a brew?

ALEC: Thank you. It's bitter out.

MAGGIE: I didn't mean for you to have to call again.

ALEC: Just checking on my patient on my way home. And I brought her this.

He puts a half bottle of whisky on the table.

MAGGIE: Whisky?

ALEC: Medicinal. A hot toddy at night will soothe the cough.

MAGGIE: How much do I…?

ALEC: Wouldn't dream of it. I was given it, by a grateful and well-heeled patient.

MAGGIE: Then you should drink it.

ALEC: No.

MAGGIE: Yes.

ALEC: Would you join me then?

MAGGIE: I don't think…

ALEC: I've had a really hard day and I don't like drinking alone. I could call in on Lorna Pepper but frankly I don't know if I've got the energy.

MAGGIE: You get used to her.

ALEC: Really?

MAGGIE: Trust me. I've lived here all my life. Just a small one then.

ALEC: What about your Gran?

MAGGIE: If she'd been pretending to sleep the word Whisky would have got her out of her chair like a shot. She's out for the count now.

ALEC: So, your husband's coming home on leave. You must be excited. Counting the days.

MAGGIE: Yeah. *(She taps her head.)* Keep touching wood nothing'll happen to stop him.

ALEC: *(Raising his glass.)* Safe home.

MAGGIE: Safe home.

ALEC: *(Moving the knitting.)* For Peg's baby?

MAGGIE: Yeah. Better go easy on this or I'll be dropping stitches.

ALEC: My father used to knit.

MAGGIE: Really?

ALEC: Said it calmed him down. He was a surgeon. Very dextrous. Good with his hands.

MAGGIE: I know what dextrous means.

ALEC: Sorry. I didn't mean to… That's what he used to do. Explain things, all the time.

MAGGIE: Passing on his knowledge to his son. It's what fathers do isn't it? And it worked, you're a doctor.

ALEC: He had very high standards.

MAGGIE: I'm sure he must be proud of you.

ALEC: What about your father?

MAGGIE: No idea. When my mum died he took off.

ALEC: I'm sorry. So…

MAGGIE: Yeah. Gran raised me.

ALEC: Maybe when you have your own children he'll…

MAGGIE: No.

ALEC: Well, you know him best…

MAGGIE: It's not that. *(Beat.)* I can't.

ALEC: Can't what, Maggie?

MAGGIE: I can't have bairns.

ALEC: Oh. I'm sorry. I didn't know.

MAGGIE: You're the only one in Keswick then.

ALEC: Surely people don't…

MAGGIE: Of course they do! I can tell you're not from round here.

Beat.

Sorry. You'd think I'd have got used to it by now.

ALEC: You've had tests?

MAGGIE: I've been married near on two years. We love each other me and Rob. There's nothing wrong with what we feel for each other. But month on month... I don't need tests to tell me if I don't fall for a baby then I'm barren. It's bloody obvious. To everyone.

ALEC: It might be something that can be sorted out. You shouldn't blame yourself.

MAGGIE: After two years of happy marriage and I'm not pregnant, who else is there to blame?

ALEC: Come on Maggie, you're a grown woman, a married woman. You must know it takes two to conceive a child.

MAGGIE: Yeah, and whoever heard of a barren man?

ALEC looks at her.

What? No. Really?

ALEC: Really.

MAGGIE: Really really?

ALEC: You've plenty of time.

MAGGIE: You're saying it might be Rob, not me?

ALEC: It's possible. It could be neither of you.

MAGGIE: What, you mean the storks are being shot down by anti-aircraft guns?

ALEC: Very likely.

MAGGIE: They do say it's been a bad year for gooseberries.

ALEC: Maggie. Just relax and stop blaming yourself, or Rob.

MAGGIE: It shouldn't make it better, you know, your saying it could just be...

ALEC: Women often fall pregnant after they've adopted. They've stopped worrying.

MAGGIE: I suppose I'm just used to thinking it's my fault.

ALEC: I see.

MAGGIE: Do you? Not just this, but everything.

ALEC: Mmn. You really shouldn't have invaded Poland.

MAGGIE: Sorry. Won't happen again. Hey, cheers.

ALEC: Cheers.

A giant weight has been lifted from MAGGIE. She knocks back her drink.

MAGGIE: Thank you. Thank you very much.

ALEC: I'll leave the rest of this here for your Gran.

MAGGIE: You going?

ALEC: I better get off home.

MAGGIE: Right.

MAGGIE picks up the whisky bottle.

MAGGIE: Thanks for this. Very generous.

ALEC: Don't give it her all at once mind.

MAGGIE: I won't. Well.

ALEC: Well.

MAGGIE: Goodnight Doctor.

ALEC: Goodnight.

MAGGIE: And…

ALEC: Yes?

MAGGIE: Nothing. *(She grins.)* Just thanks.

ALEC: Night.

ALEC leaves. MAGGIE is full of hope again.

End of scene.

Scene change song: "Sing Sing Sing"

SCENE FOUR

Church Hall. Two days later. Thursday, late morning.

There are tables set out with buns and sandwiches. Some still in the process of being made. ALEC is looking round to see where he should offload a pile of loaves and some pots of paste. LEONORE, bundled up in cardigans against the cold, waves off a student.

LEONORE: Goodbye Joanna. Try and be on time next week please.

ALEC: You've got your work cut out with that one.

LEONORE: The parents pay, the girls think piano easier than hockey in the cold.

ALEC: Bit demoralising for you though.

LEONORE: I beg your pardon?

ALEC: Teaching people who don't want to learn.

LEONORE: I also teach them German.

ALEC: The Roedean girls?

LEONORE: Ya.

ALEC: Curious choice of language – unless they're all going to grow up to be spies.

LEONORE: What other language should they learn? Italian? French?

ALEC: See your point.

LEONORE: People getting from the trains look at our class reciting German verbs in the waiting room with much suspicion.

ALEC: *(Smiling kindly.)* I expect you are used to that though.

LEONORE smiles back yes.

And there must be worst places to teach.

LEONORE: Perhaps.

She returns to the piano.

PERCE enters carrying a tray of bread and tins of Spam, followed by PEG with a large metal jug of milk.

PEG: Oh hello Doctor. God it's brass monkeys out there today isn't it? I stopped for five minutes to have a look at the hockey game in Fitz Park and my hands went numb. But then I've got terrible circulation, you should see my chilblains.

PERCE: No you shouldn't. They're horrible.

PEG clips PERCE round the head.

PEG: Perce!

PERCE: Ow!

PEG: Look at your hands!

PERCE: I've been shovelling muck.

PEG: Evidently.

PERCE: *(Nodding towards ALEC.)* Very important work, farming. Like the doctor here. Protected occupation. Dig for victory. Use spades not ships.

PEG: Thank you Perce.

PERCE: Lend a Hand on the Land.

PEG: Perce enough!

PERCE: Oh right. Where d'you want these?

HILDA and MAGGIE enter from the back. LEONORE is playing "Moonlight Sonata" quietly.

MAGGIE: Oh hello. Over there please Perce. Have you got time to have a look at that wonky table while you're here? Sorry Doctor, they can go on the end over there. How're you?

ALEC: Fine thanks. Yourself? You're looking well despite all this.

MAGGIE: Well the drivers need feeding and we do know how to feed people.

PEG: And our Rob's coming home on leave any minute. After months and months away. She should really've stayed home to get ready for him.

MAGGIE: I am ready. Who sent this?

ALEC: I called in at Lorna's and she asked if I could drop them off on my way.

MAGGIE: Did she now? And what's she carrying?

ALEC: She said she'd be along later.

MAGGIE: She's supposed to be in charge now, not later! We'll have forty drivers in here lunchtime, the urn's on the frizz, the pipes are frozen and if I hear The Moonlight Sonata one more time I'll scream.

PEG: Why don't you play something English Leonore? For a change.

LEONORE starts to play "White Cliffs Of Dover".

And now there's the concert to organise.

MAGGIE: Well that is definitely her job. I don't care what her excuse is. Urns I can deal with but I draw the line at artistic temperaments. Hilda love if I cut can you make a start on these? Just a scraping, this paste has to go a long way. So, what is her excuse?

Holding the loaf to her chest, MAGGIE starts to cut slices.

ALEC: She says her son's not well.

MAGGIE: Has she called you in for a consultation?

ALEC: No. I don't think it's that bad.

MAGGIE: No I don't suppose it is.

PEG: Probably still got a hangover from last Saturday.

PERCE: Can you hold onto this a minute Doctor?

ALEC steadies the table for PERCE.

MAGGIE: Poor old Charlie made a proper Charlie of himself.

PEG: He is a laugh.

MAGGIE: *(Looking at her.)* Yeah.

PEG: It was funny.

MAGGIE grins at her, teasing.

MAGGIE: You clearly thought so.

PEG: Shut up you.

ALEC: Must be hard being an only son.

PEG: Why d'you say that Doctor?

MAGGIE: It's no bed of roses being an only anything.

PEG: Have you got brothers and sisters?

ALEC: Sisters. Yes.

PEG: I bet they dote on you.

PERCE: You don't dote on me.

PEG: No. I've got Rob for that. You're for company. And fixing things.

PERCE: It's good to be useful. Keep Calm and Carry On.

ALEC: Quite right. How's your Gran?

MAGGIE: Fit as a flea, thanks. Has anyone seen her lately?

PEG: She was in a queue outside Bordens with Dolly Lattimer. She'll be fine.

MAGGIE: Till she gets to the front and hasn't a glimmer what she's there for.

PEG: So? She'll just go to the back and start again. Or someone'll bring her over. Stop worrying.

MAGGIE looks round.

MAGGIE: Oh no. Who's been at these cakes?

PEG: I just got here.

PEG looks pointedly at LEONORE.

MAGGIE: Four glace cherries they've taken. I've been saving those for months. Was it those blooming evacuees, pardon my French?

She looks at HILDA who says nothing.

MAGGIE: Hilda? You'll not be telling tales.

HILDA says nothing.

I thought we were supposed to be pulling together.

PERCE finishes fixing the table leg.

PERCE: There you go. Right as rain.

MAGGIE: Thanks Perce.

PERCE: How was the rabbit pie?

MAGGIE: Lovely. Did I not thank you before?

PERCE: I've cleaned the fur, for your Jean. Is she coming in?

MAGGIE: No she's working. Though how she manages it on the three hours sleep she had last night I've no idea. And before you ask, I don't know where she was. Just out.

PERCE: Oh. D'you know when…?

MAGGIE: If you're determined, you could try around six tonight.

PERCE: That's Home Guard. We're doing cocktails.

PEG: You what?

PERCE: I don't think it's to sup.

PEG: Why not?

PERCE: It requires petrol.

PEG: Heaven help us.

PERCE: Be fair, Peg. We've had no accidents to date.

ALEC: That's not what the man I treated on Saturday said.

PERCE: That would have been Workington, right? Not us. Not Keswick.

PEG: You never said.

ALEC: Peaceful afternoon at the pictures was all he expected.

MAGGIE: What happened?

ALEC: Apparently they had a call out that an enemy parachute'd been seen coming down.

PERCE: They were issued with five rounds of ammo. Imagine that! Five rounds!

ALEC: But they couldn't find any sign of the airman

PERCE: Be fair. It was dark by then and a lot of ground to cover. Sorry. Go on.

ALEC: No. You. You'll tell it better Perce.

PERCE: You reckon, Doctor?

PEG: Get on with it!

PERCE: Anyroad they eventually give up and come back to their base in the cellar of the cinema, possibly a bit overexcited and fed up they've missed most of the John Wayne picture on upstairs and then well, one of the lads – no one's saying who – lets off all five rounds through the ceiling. Upstairs in the cinema this bloke leaps from his seat shouting "I've been shot! I've been shot!" and everyone tells him to sit down and shut up it's only a cowboy flick till they see he's got blood pouring out his trouser leg. Laugh! He is going to be all right, isn't he Doctor?

ALEC's on his way out.

ALEC: As rain. Once the stitches are out and he can walk again, yes. Terrific.

MAGGIE laughs.

MAGGIE: Sorry. I'm sure he doesn't find it funny.

ALEC exits. MAGGIE and PEG watch him go.

PEG: Wrap up warm! It's going to snow again.

MAGGIE: "Wrap up warm" – who are you, his mother?

PEG: *(Giggling.)* If only I wasn't married.

PERCE: See you teatime.

PERCE exits. PEG waves.

MAGGIE: And expecting… bye Perce.

PEG: Well, he makes a change from old Dr Beasley. They say Keswick's never had so many women feeling under the weather.

MAGGIE: He's a very kind man. Gentle.

PEG: I think your Jean's got her eye on him.

MAGGIE: You might have been right about that last week. But as of this morning she's in love with that boy she met at the tea dance. Trainee pilot over at Millom.

PEG: I can't work out if she's fast or fun. What d'you think?

MAGGIE: Being neither how the heck would I know?

PEG: I think you're fun. Well you would be if you'd sing with us.

MAGGIE: Not a chance. Musicality skipped a generation and went off for pie and chips when it saw me coming. Gran and my mother got all that was on offer. Nothing left for me.

PEG: Oh come on. Nobody's going to judge you.

MAGGIE: Excuse me, that's exactly what they're going to do! Stand up in front of a whole crowd of people and make a fool of myself? What kind of clown d'you take me for?

PEG: It'll be fun.

MAGGIE: Like the time you let me walk all the way up Station Road with my dress tucked in my knickers?

PEG moves towards the piano.

PEG: Have you got another pupil coming Leonore?

LEONORE: Not till 11.

PEG: Why don't I play something then, cheer us all up.

LEONORE: What would you like?

PEG: I'd like to sit at the piano.

LEONORE gestures to a chair nearby. PEG ignores it.

LEONORE: How about this?

She plays "White Cliffs Of Dover".

Do you like this one?

PEG: No. Everyone'll do that.

LEONORE tries "Lily Marlene".

LEONORE: This would suit your voice.

PEG: I've said before. Too German.

MAGGIE: Red Robin?

LEONORE: I don't know this.

PEG: I do!

She sweeps LEONORE off the piano chair and launches into "The Red Red Robin".

PEG: *(After one verse.)* Come on you lot!

Hilda, I bet you know this.

Singing.

MAGGIE: Go on love.

HILDA joins in singing.

Leonore?

LEONORE takes her knitting out of her bag, a beautiful piece of intricate knitwork.

LEONORE: *(Shaking her head.)* I'm nearly there now.

MAGGIE: I wish I could knit like that. I don't know how you do it.

LEONORE: Years at practice.

MAGGIE: Who's it for?

LEONORE: My sister.

MAGGIE: In Germany?

LEONORE: I hope no longer.

MAGGIE: Have you heard…?

LEONORE: No.

MAGGIE: Well they say no news is good news.

PEG: We need a third for the lower part. Come on Maggie.

MAGGIE: I can't.

PEG: Rubbish. Hilda, you and Maggie take the tune and I'll do the harmony. Two three!

HILDA takes MAGGIE's hand to pull her in towards the piano. Reluctantly MAGGIE joins in. Unseen by them GRAN enters followed by PERCE and finally ROB looking gorgeous in his RAF uniform. They watch the trio give a rousing if amateur rendition. At the end LEONORE, ROB, PERCE and GRAN applaud.

PEG: I think we've got a trio girls!

MAGGIE: *(Seeing GRAN first.)* Oh Gran, where've you been?

PERCE: *(Beaming, presenting ROB.)* Look who I found.

PEG turns and sees her brother and hurls herself across the room at him.

PEG: Rob!

He swings her round and puts her down.

47

ROB: Hello sis.

He looks at MAGGIE, smiling.

Maggie?

MAGGIE: You're early. I meant to dress up.

ROB: You don't need to.

They embrace. Over her shoulder ROB sees HILDA watching them, stony faced. He smiles.

ROB: And you must be Hilda.

HILDA stares back at him, silent. GRAN looks up from the sandwiches she's munching, one in either hand.

GRAN: Mm fish paste. My favourite. Are we expecting company?

End of scene.

Scene change song: "Hold Tight" [Andrews Sisters]

SCENE FIVE

MAGGIE's kitchen. 5 days later, Tuesday morning.

Several days later. The airer above the stove is hung with hanks of recycled wool. On the table is a large preserving pan full of hedgerow fruit. On the floor is a basket full of balls of recycled wool. HILDA is reading a book. GRAN knits by the fire. JEAN is creating minor chaos searching for her gloves etc to go off to work. PERCE nervously gulps at his cup of tea and burns his mouth. He says nothing

JEAN: Are you all right?

PERCE: *(Lying.)* Fine.

JEAN: So are you going in for the concert party?

PERCE: Thought I might.

She searches round GRAN's knitting for her gloves.

GRAN: Whatever you're wanting you'll not find it under there. It's for tanks.

JEAN: Sorry Mrs S. I know my gloves are around somewhere.

GRAN: You should have them on elastic. That's what I did with our Maggie.

JEAN: Never mind gloves. If I could lay my hands on elastic I'd use it to keep my drawers up.

PERCE gulps and burns himself on the tea again.

JEAN: You sure you're all right? You look a bit pink.

PERCE: Fine.

JEAN: I hear you do bird impressions.

PERCE: That's right.

JEAN: What can you do?

PERCE: Anything you like. Nightingale, tit, warbler, red finch.

He purses his lips and makes a bird noise.

JEAN: Amazing. What's that?

PERCE: Warbler.

He makes another identical bird noise.

JEAN: And that?

PERCE: Nightingale.

He makes another identical bird noise.

Red finch.

He makes another identical bird noise.

PERCE: Tit.

GRAN sings a couple of lines of "Tit Willow" in a clear sweet voice.

GRAN: Many many tits.

JEAN laughs. PERCE doesn't know where to put himself and, covered in embarassment, knocking into furniture on the way, he leaves.

GRAN: He was always a strange boy. Had a habit of picking his nose and sticking the bogies on the wall by his bed.

JEAN: I do wish you hadn't told me that Mrs S. Whew that chicken mess smells disgusting.

GRAN: Chickens!

Singing 'Tit Willow' to herself, she picks up the chicken mash bucket, gets into her wellies and goes out into the yard. JEAN sees that GRAN has been sitting on her gloves.

JEAN: Mustn't grumble. Nice and warm.

MAGGIE and ROB enter as she shrugs into her coat and hat.

Hello lovebirds! Sorry, can't stop. My turn on the tractor today! Watch out Keswick!

JEAN ruffles HILDA's hair.

Tara pet.

To ROB.

JEAN: I'm learning Geordie. Bit of a way to go yet. Wye aye!

JEAN swishes out, inadvertently swiping ROB with her scarf as she flicks it over her shoulder.

MAGGIE: Bye Jean. See you later. You in for tea?

JEAN: Yes please! I'll cut your fringe for you then, okay?

MAGGIE: Grand. Bye love.

ROB: The longer I'm home the more it feels like being at a girl's boarding school!

MAGGIE feels the teapot and fills it up from the kettle on the stove. Pours ROB's tea and puts it down on the table.

MAGGIE: There are those who'd think that an advantage.

ROB sits down at the table. On his chair is a bag of LEONORE's knitting. He has a look at it.

ROB: You've come on a bit.

MAGGIE: Fancy you noticing.

She gives him a kiss.

I've not got past socks. That's Leonore's knitting, she must have left it behind last night. Beautiful isn't it? Work of art. Hope in every stitch.

ROB wants to prolong the kiss but MAGGIE nods towards HILDA watching in the corner.

MAGGIE: You're going to be late for school, Hilda. She does love her books.

ROB: What're you reading pet?

HILDA shows him the cover.

MAGGIE: Cat got your tongue? It's only my Rob, he's harmless.

ROB: Thanks very much.

MAGGIE serves him with porridge, puts on honey.

MAGGIE: Tastes almost as good as sugar.

MAGGIE bustles around helping HILDA on with her coat, hat, gloves etc.

Oh my. We're going to have to put a border on these sleeves. Either that or you'll have to stop growing. Hilda's a real help to me these days. Aren't you love? Gloves? Good. Pull this down properly over your ears it's freezing out.

HILDA points to MAGGIE's apron pocket.

HILDA: My mum.

MAGGIE: *(Taking out an opened letter, smiling.)* Nothing gets past you does it? Yeah she wrote to me. Everything's fine.

Don't worry. I'll see you dinnertime. I'll be at the centre, all right? Call in and we'll walk back together. I'm sure I'll have something to carry so I'll need your strong arms. Off you go now. Be good.

ROB: Bye Hilda.

HILDA acknowledges him with a small nod and, giving him a wide berth, leaves.

Whew that's a relief!

MAGGIE: Oh she's all right. She'll get used to you.

ROB: Don't know as I'll get used to being watched all the time.

MAGGIE: All creatures like you. You'll have to give her time.

ROB: What little time I've got is reserved for my wife.

MAGGIE: Don't say that.

ROB: Why not?

MAGGIE: I don't know. Sounds like you're going to die.

ROB: No one's killing me off Maggie. I won't let them. And what I meant was the time I've got home on leave is all yours.

MAGGIE: Yeah.

ROB: I thought we could go skating on the lake.

MAGGIE: We haven't got any skates.

ROB: We could borrow some. Someone'll have a pair or two.

MAGGIE: Why don't you ask around, see what you can find while I'm at work...

ROB: Work?

MAGGIE: Then if there's time this afternoon...

ROB: You're not going to the centre again today are you?

MAGGIE: I've got to. They need me.

ROB: You told me you had Lorna Lady Muck in charge.

MAGGIE: Supposed to be, but she's never there.

ROB: That's not your problem.

MAGGIE: The drivers won't get their lunch, the woollens won't get sorted, given out to the knitters. I feel responsible.

ROB: Maggie, they're not even paying you!

MAGGIE: I don't need paying. We can manage. Government gives us a bit for Jean.

ROB: Bet that doesn't even cover the electric.

MAGGIE: I put money aside for that, like you told me. I'm managing. And Jean's fun. We go out, have a laugh.

ROB: Sounds like you've got everything sorted.

MAGGIE: *(Not picking up the cue.)* Sometimes I surprise myself. Who'd have thought it? And we get something for Hilda as well. I meant to talk to you about that.

ROB: What about?

MAGGIE: This letter from her mum…

ROB: She must be missing her.

MAGGIE: Well…thing is…

ROB: Don't tell me she wants to come and live here too? Does she know it's like a wool factory?

MAGGIE: Give over.

She smiles and gives him a kiss on the forehead.

Actually she's not missing her at all.

ROB: Poor kid.

MAGGIE: I know. I think she's settled really well, under the circumstances. Some of them, like Peg's Sidney, are little devils, wet the bed and all sorts of carry on. Not Hilda.

She turns so he can't see her face.

More tea?

He moves his mug towards her.

Thing is she's written asking if we'd keep her on. You know, afterwards. Imagine your own mother not wanting you. I mean, I know she's happy here – she shows me her letters home. One of them said "It's Autumn now. They have Autumn every year in Keswick." Imagine. And she's really excited about Peg's baby. Well we all are. Just think, you're going to be an uncle.

ROB: That's it, rub it in.

MAGGIE: What?

ROB: Suppose it's the next best thing to being a father.

MAGGIE: I didn't mean that at all.

ROB: What did you mean then? You want me to take on some stranger's brat cos you can't have one of your own.

MAGGIE: I'm just telling you what she asked.

ROB: Well she can ask all she likes. I don't like it.

MAGGIE: Okay. I was just saying.

ROB: Don't put that face on.

MAGGIE: I'm not putting on any face. I just hoped we might talk about it.

ROB: What's to talk about?

MAGGIE: Instead of dismissing it out of hand.

ROB: I'm not...oh who am I kidding? You decide. You seem to make all the decisions in this house now.

MAGGIE: Only while you're not here.

ROB: So it's my fault now is it? I'm away serving my country and like to get shot to pieces in flames for the privilege, seeing my mates going off and not coming back, knowing that could be me next time, while you're here gallivanting out of a night, having a laugh, house full of waifs and strays and this is all my fault?

MAGGIE: I never said that. There is a war on here too you know.

ROB: Oh I can see that. Air raids, bombs, fires. You've got it really tough. Do you listen to the news at all, what's happening in London, what's happening in France?

MAGGIE: Of course I do.

ROB: You have no idea what it's like.

MAGGIE: I know I worry myself sleepless about all the people dying and having no homes, and kids being burned and you not coming back.

ROB: So?

MAGGIE: I can't alter that. But every driver I serve a dinner to down the canteen is you, every pair of socks I knit for some unknown seaman is for you…

ROB: And every man in uniform at the dances you go to for a laugh, is he me too?

MAGGIE: No, because they wouldn't talk to me like that.

ROB lashes out and hits her on the face.

MAGGIE: I'm sorry.

ROB: Oh Maggie, don't say that. It's me. I'm so sorry. Please love.

MAGGIE: It's okay.

ROB: No it's not. I'm sorry. I don't know what came over me. Your poor face. I'm so sorry.

MAGGIE: Yeah, yeah you said.

He tries to help her.

No. No I'm all right. Really. I'll say I walked into a lamp post. With the blackout, everyone's doing it.

He gets some cold water on tea towel.

ROB: Here. Shall I get some snow?

MAGGIE: I'll be all right.

ROB puts his head in his hands, then slams his fist on the table. MAGGIE flinches.

ROB: I'm so scared Maggie. All the time. Everyone talks about our brave lads, our brave soldiers. Whoever they are, I'm not one of them. I just want to stay alive. I want to come home. I've been counting the days, the minutes to be back here, in our kitchen with you, safe, here, together. But you're not. Not the same. You're changing. The whole world's shifting and I'm afraid I'm just going to fall off.

MAGGIE: *(Hugging him.)* I'll still be here when you come back.

ROB: Looking down from the aircraft, you realise we aren't even specs of sand, we're dust – little heaps of dust hiding under houses and shelters. We don't mean anything.

MAGGIE: It'll be all right. You'll come home. You will. And we may not have any pots and pans left, and be living on grass but we'll be here. Waiting.

She comforts him.

Sssh, ssh. It's all right. Fill up the kettle. Wash your face, have a shave. You'll feel better then.

ROB takes the kettle and exits. HILDA enters followed by PERCE.

HILDA: Aunty Maggie!

MAGGIE: What're you doing back?

HILDA: I forgot my knitting for the sailors, and then I…

MAGGIE: Well what do you expect me to do? I can't do everything for you all the time for God's sake! Go and look for it!

HILDA, shocked, runs off.

I'm sorry. Sorry. I didn't mean to shout. But sometimes I can't, you know, I just can't…take… Fine mother I'd make. No patience at all. Still, no point in grumbling about it. I suppose you'll be wanting a brew then Perce?

PERCE: Er no.

MAGGIE: What's up, you feeling poorly?

PERCE: I feel dreadful.

MAGGIE: Oh dear. You think it's the flu?

PERCE: No. It were the cocktails. I were practising. I wanted to get it right.

MAGGIE: Sit down, I'll get you a cold flannel

PERCE: No I can't. You don't understand. It's on fire.

MAGGIE: If you haven't got the head for it, Perce…

PERCE: It's not me.

MAGGIE: They made you drink, did they?

PERCE: No! You got to come quickly. Now. It's not me, it's the hall that's on fire.

End of Act One.

Song: "Be Like The Kettle And Sing"

Act Two

Song: "Be Like The Kettle And Sing"

SCENE ONE

Next day. Wednesday afternoon.

They are cleaning up the fire damage, and more importantly water damage, with mops and buckets, brushes and cloths. Lines are strung across the room with donated clothes drying on them. Present are PEG, HILDA, PERCE, MAGGIE – with a bruise on her face – ROB, ALEC, LEONORE, and GRAN. ROB helps LEONORE move the piano so he can mop behind it. She smiles at him. He has a knack of making people feel at ease. Four evacuees, all wearing sooty face decoration, are playing cowboys and indians.

ROB: Is here okay? Careful, don't hurt your back. Let me do it. Ok?

LEONORE: Thank you.

ROB: It looks odd seeing it down here.

LEONORE: You don't mind?

ROB: Pianos don't mean anything if there's nobody playing them.

LEONORE: Thank goodness it is not burned.

PEG: Oh yes, thank goodness for that. As long as the Swanky Rodents can have their piano lessons everything's all right with the world.

ROB imitates her, sending her up. She grins.

Oh shut up.

Where do you want these putting Maggie?

MAGGIE: Are they wet?

PEG: Everything in the back room's wet.

MAGGIE: Hang them up with the rest. I suppose they'll dry out eventually.

GRAN, knitting, starts to sing "Hang Out The Washing On The Siegfried Line".

PEG: The fire would have probably gone out in the snow but oh no, they had to hose fifty million gallons in here as well.

PERCE: *(Up a stepladder fixing up drying lines.)* Sorry.

PEG: Don't even start with sorry.

MAGGIE: Cocktails, I ask you.

PEG: What were you thinking?

PERCE: I wanted to impress her.

PEG: Who?

PERCE: Jean.

PEG: Dear God.

PERCE: Thought she'd see me like a commando. You know...

He mimes Lighting the Molotov cocktail, throwing it and ducking.

Cover!

PEG: You idiot.

PERCE: I weren't aiming at the hall. That were an accident.

PEG: You're an accident.

PERCE: I've got a new idea now. For the concert party.

PEG: Is it flammable?

PERCE: I hope not.

PERCE checks his pockets. MAGGIE smiles, he's told her about his magic tricks. There's a crash off.

Peg: Oh my god. Sidney!

PEG exits to the back.

MAGGIE: *(To the evacuees.)* And you lot. Out of here. Come along, you're not helping.

MAGGIE shoos the evacuees off. They run round her.

In the name of…where the hell is Lorna Pepper when there's work to be done?

LEONORE: She said she'd be here.

ROB gets onto his mop and rounds them up and, firing an imaginary gun, chases them out. He smiles over at MAGGIE. She smiles back but there's distance between them.

ALEC: I see war paint is in fashion for both cowboys and Indians.

ROB: Any excuse to get really filthy.

LEONORE: Mrs Pepper is putting on her boots when I leave the house.

MAGGIE: Well I won't hold my breath. How does it sound? Has water got into it?

LEONORE: So you do care about it after all?

MAGGIE: It's the only heirloom I've got. Apart from Gran of course. Must count for something I suppose.

LEONORE: Well, of course. It belonged to your mother who loved it.

MAGGIE: Oh yes, she loved that piano all right. OK everyone, we need to keep this end clear for the soup and sandwiches. There's still a war on and stomachs'll still rumble come dinnertime.

MAGGIE and LEONORE move tables together.

ALEC: She's amazing, your Maggie, never stops.

ROB: Yeah I'd noticed. I'd quite like her to actually. It's not long before I'm due back.

ALEC: I envy you.

ROB: What, me wife?

ALEC: No. I mean, she's a wonderful woman but I meant being able to do your bit.

ROB: Well, if there's one thing all the services need it's medics.

ALEC: Not with asthma. Be a liability. I've tried. Several times. No one'll have me.

ROB: From what I hear on the QT you get your share of trainee pilots round here need fixing up.

ALEC: If only. It's usually too late for anything I have to offer

ROB understands he means fatalities.

ROB: So, you like it here?

ALEC: What's not to like? Good beer, beautiful countryside, good beer.

ROB grins.

ROB: Me and Perce're going to the George later. Fancy a beer to get the soot out of our throats?

ALEC: Thought you'd never ask!

JEAN enters muffled up.

JEAN: Ask what?

ROB: It's man's talk Jean.

JEAN: Beer or football? If it's the former can I come too?

MAGGIE: Rob, could you be a love and pop down to Lorna Pepper's, ask where she's hidden the key to the store cupboard? Jean, what're you doing here?

ROB leaves.

JEAN: Everything's frozen solid. Been seconded to help you. My idea. Jolly good one too, you've got a lovely fug going in here. Hello Perce, you old arsonist.

PERCE: It were an accident.

JEAN: That's what they all say.

PERCE: Who does?

JEAN: Never mind. How're the bird impressions coming along? Not long to go till the concert.

MAGGIE: He's branched out, haven't you Perce?

PERCE: Magic.

JEAN: Really?

PERCE: Hang on.

PERCE gets out his pack of cards and shuffles them about, breathing heavily as he concentrates.

JEAN: I thought you'd all be singing while you worked. Blackout Stroll sounded pretty good this morning.

MAGGIE: You weren't listening?

JEAN: *(Muttering.)* Better than the song of the lesser spotted nightingale.

Gran, still knitting her tank camouflage starts to sing in the background "And A Nightingale Sang In Berkeley Square".

PERCE holds out a fan of cards.

PERCE: Pick a card. Any card.

JEAN does so.

Now look at it. Don't tell me what it is.

JEAN: Wasn't going to.

PERCE: Now then. Was it... *(Convinced he's right.)* ...The two of diamonds!

JEAN: No.

PERCE: Oh. Okay then, *(Still confident.)* was it the four of diamonds?

JEAN: No.

PERCE: Eight?

> *JEAN shakes her head.*

Ten?

> *JEAN shakes her head.*

PERCE: Any diamond?

JEAN: 'Fraid not.

PERCE: You sure?

JEAN: Positive. It's the…

PERCE: No, don't tell me. Is it…the…?

MAGGIE: Why don't you take the weight off? This could take an awfully long time.

PERCE: I know, two of clubs!

JEAN: No.

PERCE: Hearts? Spades? It must be yan of them!

> *LEONORE has picked up her knitting bag and looking inside makes a small cry.*

MAGGIE: What's up?

LEONORE: My knitting.

MAGGIE: It's not got wet has it?

> *LEONORE looks around, shocked.*

Leonore? What is it? Oh no.

> *She pulls out what's left of the back of the jumper, a mass of unravelled wool pulled off the needles*

Who'd do a thing like that? It was so beautiful.

> *PEG enters.*

PEG: What? What's everyone looking at?

MAGGIE: Leonore, I'm so sorry.

LEONORE: These things happen.

MAGGIE: Not here.

LEONORE: Everywhere.

GRAN is still singing. ROB enters from the street. Looks at ALEC.

MAGGIE: Okay, where is she then? What's her excuse this time?

ROB puts his hand on MAGGIE's arm.

MAGGIE: What?

ROB: I'm afraid she's had some bad news.

MAGGIE: What sort of…

ROB: Telegram.

MAGGIE: Not Charlie?

ROB: Yes. Killed in action.

MAGGIE turns to ROB.

PEG: *(Bursting into tears.)* But he was only here the other weekend.

LEONORE gets up to leave.

MAGGIE: Leonore, are you all right?

PEG: Why are you worried about her?

MAGGIE: Peg, please.

LEONORE: I'll take care of her.

PEG: That'll be a big comfort. If it hadn't been for you people her son'd still be alive!

LEONORE starts to leave.

ROB: Peg. Enough!

ALEC: Let me come with you.

LEONORE shakes him off.

LEONORE: I'm all right.

PEG: He's not talking about you!

ALEC: Maggie if you could get her some hot sweet tea. She's had a shock. We all have. I'll be along soon.

MAGGIE: Of course.

He puts a hand on LEONORE's arm. She nods and leaves.

PEG: Why don't you go back where you belong. Bloody Nazis!

ALEC: Her family were arrested for sheltering a Jewish family. She hasn't heard from them since.

MAGGIE: Come on love.

PEG: I'm not a mean person.

MAGGIE: Of course you're not.

PEG: But Charlie... I was dancing with him, flicking those stupid taxi door ears of his. Those poor ears.

GRAN: Last time I watched all the young lads in our village march bravely off to war. Only one came back and he was broken. That's what war is, young people dying, other people mourning them, same all over the world. Can't afford to get too sentimental. This isn't over yet, Peg, not by a long chalk.

End of scene.

Scene change song: "Wish Me Luck"

SCENE TWO

Five days later. Monday late afternoon.

MAGGIE and HILDA are painting and wiring fir cones for Christmas decorations. GRAN is dozing by the fire. ROB enters.

MAGGIE: You fixed it?

ROB: Well I've done the best I could. How they can call a ball-cock non-essential is beyond me.

MAGGIE: Far as I'm concerned a functioning lavvy is the best Christmas present a woman could wish for.

ROB: I'll say this for you Maggie, you don't demand much.

MAGGIE: No?

ROB: You just get on with it.

MAGGIE: I like keeping busy. Learning new things.

ROB: Come out back and I'll show you how I fixed it then shall I?

MAGGIE: I'm sure, fingers crossed, it'll be fine.

ROB: You'd have a job doing that with your fingers crossed.

MAGGIE: Oh I don't know. I've become very dextrous these days. It means good with your

ROB: Hands. Yeah, I know. I'm not stupid.

MAGGIE: *(Hearing the door.)* That'll be Jean.

ROB: Ready to put some other poor bloke's head on a platter.

MAGGIE: Oh don't be so daft. She's a very popular girl.

ROB: I wonder why. Poor sods.

MAGGIE: Excuse me, there's a child in the room. Come on Hilda, let's go and see if the chickens have got any eggs for us today.

MAGGIE and HILDA exit to the garden. JEAN and LEONORE enter.

JEAN: Come in and sit down. There. I'll pour us a cuppa. Pot's still warm.

ROB: I'd rather have a drink.

JEAN: No can do, old fruit. Shame. I'm sure Leonore could do with one too.

ROB: Why's that?

JEAN: I found her sitting at the bus stop, shaking, poor old sausage. So I scooped her up and brought her home. ...to Maggie's, your place.

ROB: What's up?

JEAN: Some stupid fancy dress prank the Rodean girls pulled. Two of them dressed up as Nazis and marched up and down the station platform.

ROB: What!

LEONORE: They thought it was funny.

JEAN: Idiots. You mustn't let it upset you.

LEONORE: Upset? I want to kill them. Up against the wall and shoot.

JEAN: *(Shocked.)* Okay.

LEONORE: They are just children. Stupid girls...

ROB: Nevertheless

LEONORE: Nevertheless I want to shoot them.

JEAN: You should say something. Make a fuss.

LEONORE: I have nowhere else to go. I need my job. No I will keep my eyes down and my mouth shut, just like so many of my countrymen. I thought I was different.

JEAN: That makes me so angry.

LEONORE: Yes, me also.

JEAN: When I think of the money wasted educating those idiots to a state where they think it's okay to dress up as Nazis for a bit of fun – when I think of all the books, all the teachers, all that could do for kids like Hilda and Sidney – well maybe not Sidney but you know what I mean. It just makes me want to stamp. It really does.

ROB: Well well...

JEAN: God, if Daddy could hear me he'd cut me off without a penny. But it's not right. And it's not fair.

ROB: Hear hear. So, will we make a socialist of you yet?

JEAN: Steady on. I wouldn't go that far.

ROB: One step at a time?

JEAN: Long as it's not a goose step. I think I better go and get changed. Got a bit hot under the collar, and all points south.

JEAN exits.

LEONORE: She's a good girl.

ROB: Good?

LEONORE: Kind.

ROB: I suppose she's all right, for a toff.

LEONORE: Since the last three years I have kindness from people I would never have dreamed of being part of my world. I have learned to trust what people do, not what they say.

ROB: Fair enough. *(Beat.)* I've got to go back tonight.

LEONORE: Tonight? Does Maggie know this?

ROB: I wanted to protect her.

LEONORE: By keeping her in ignorance?

ROB: I can't bear goodbyes.

LEONORE: But you must bear it. It may be all she has.

ROB: Woah there, you don't pull your punches do you?

LEONORE: I don't understand?

ROB: You're saying I might not come back.

LEONORE: Of course. This is war. Not picnics. And I think you said it was Maggie who needs protecting?

ROB: Now that was below the belt. Tell you what, I'd kill for a drink. Do you want to come to the pub?

LEONORE gives him a look.

Okay bad idea. Next time I'm home on leave?

LEONORE: I will be delighted.

GRAN approaches with the remainder of the half bottle of whisky.

GRAN: I can't get the glasses.

ROB: Whisky? Gran you old treasure.

MAGGIE and HILDA enter.

MAGGIE: Look what our ladies laid for us. Show them Hilda.

HILDA displays an egg in either hand.

ROB: Amazing.

MAGGIE: Two perfect eggs. You shall have them for your breakfast.

ROB: Er… No.

MAGGIE: There's nothing wrong with them.

ROB: *(Looking at LEONORE.)* I er I have to leave tonight.

Beat.

MAGGIE: Then I'll cook them for you now.

ROB: No. Maggie? I didn't want to spoil the day.

MAGGIE: So you spent it mending the ball cock.

ROB: House full of people, you need a functioning…

MAGGIE: How about how I wanted to spend the day?

ROB: We were just going to have a drink.

LEONORE: I must go.

ROB: No. Stay. Gran's been hiding this bottle of whisky. God knows where she got it from. Where'd you get this Gran?

GRAN: Doctor brought it for Maggie.

ROB: Alec?

MAGGIE: He brought it for you Gran, for your chest.

GRAN: No.

MAGGIE: Yes.

GRAN: So why did you and him sit here in the dark drinking it then?

MAGGIE: He had one drink on his way home after a bad day. You'll get me a bad reputation Gran.

She turns to ROB smiling.

MAGGIE: We thought she was asleep.

She sees the look on ROB's face.

Oh come on! He's the doctor! Rob?

LEONORE: Rob? Rob. I have to say goodbye now.

ROB: What? Okay, goodbye.

LEONORE: Let me look at you smiling so I remember you this way until the next time we meet.

ROB gets control of his feelings and smiles.

ROB: Yeah. *(Beat.)* I owe you a drink.

LEONORE: Who knows? I may owe you everything I care about. Look after yourself. We will take care of Maggie. Goodbye.

LEONORE leaves. MAGGIE puts her arms round ROB.

MAGGIE: Oh Rob. You'll miss the concert and everything.

ROB: Bugger the concert. I'll miss you.

ROB holds her tight. They kiss. GRAN takes HILDA's clenched hands towards the saucer where she lets go of the crushed eggs.

GRAN: Go on, let go. Now go wash your hands and while they're carrying on we'll pick out the bits of shell together.

End of scene.

Scene change song: "I'll Be Seeing You"

SCENE THREE

MAGGIE's kitchen. 3 days later. Thursday late afternoon.

The wireless is playing Christmas songs. GRAN is singing along, holding a hank of wool while HILDA winds it into a ball.

GRAN: You're good at this aren't you?

HILDA runs round GRAN with the wool, tying her up.

Like a parcel. A Christmas parcel. What do you hope for for Christmas dearie?

HILDA shakes her head. Not telling.

GRAN: Me too.

HILDA hears voices off of MAGGIE and PEG and quickly untangles GRAN and retreats to the shadows by the fire.

PEG and MAGGIE enter all wrapped up and glowing from the cold and carrying old fashioned skates.

MAGGIE: You should have come Hilda. It was such fun! Sidney was skating holding onto a chair to keep him upright.

PEG: Lord knows where he got it.

MAGGIE has a quick look round.

PEG: Even Sidney wouldn't be that stupid. It's funny you know, this [the baby] has made me feel quite affectionate. Even to him. Just think, this time next year I'll have a pram to keep me upright on the ice.

MAGGIE: Always assuming the lake freezes over again.

PEG: Alf can teach him to skate.

MAGGIE: Round in circles?

PEG: Probably. Seems funny with Rob gone.

MAGGIE: Yeah. Seemed funny when he was here too.

PEG: How d'you mean?

MAGGIE: Oh nothing. Nothing's the same anymore is it?

PEG: You haven't had words?

MAGGIE: No. But yesterday I found myself standing in the snow, reading that memorial to Lance Corporal John Strong. Over and over. Couldn't tear myself away.

PEG: What?

MAGGIE: "He whom this scroll commemorates was numbered among those who, at the call of King and Country, left all that was dear to them, endured hardness, faced danger, and finally passed out of the sight of men by the path of duty and self-sacrifice, giving up their own lives that others might live in freedom. Let those who come after see to it that his name be not forgotten"

PEG: We'll not forget Charlie.

MAGGIE: That's what Alec said.

PEG: Alec?

MAGGIE: I'd been stood there for hours. I was getting morbid. And cold. He was kind. That's all. So, Alf's a happy man. Any chance of him coming home on leave?

PEG: Soon hopefully. Though if he does he'll want to wrap us in cotton wool. I told him, I'm having a good time while I can, keep our spirits up with a bit of singing and dancing. Time enough for stopping home by the fire when I've a wain on my lap. So Hilda, you been practising?

MAGGIE: We're not very good. Hilda's learnt her part but I'm a bit of a let down.

PEG: Shall we have a go? Eh? Let's get it right together then we'll do the harmony.

They start to sing "The Blackout Stroll". HILDA doesn't join in.

Come on Hilda! What's up with you?

HILDA says nothing.

MAGGIE: She's got a bit of a sore throat.

PEG: Okay let's just do our parts then.

As they sing they start to impro a stroll dance. ALEC enters and watches smiling then applauds.

ALEC: Bravo! Well done!

MAGGIE is overcome with embarrassment and PEG glows and flutters.

PEG: Well thank you, kind sir.

MAGGIE: No one's supposed to see us yet.

ALEC: Sorry. It sounded such fun I didn't want to interrupt.

MAGGIE: Just silliness. We probably won't do that anyway.

PEG: We shall too. D'you think we should? I think we should.

MAGGIE laughs at her.

MAGGIE: Peg!

PEG: What?

MAGGIE: You're talking for two.

PEG: Yeah well I'm allowed in my condition. Isn't that so?

ALEC: Definitely. I hope you don't mind but I thought you might have some use for these. They're from one of my patients. I think they're mostly baby things.

PEG: Oh they're lovely. Aaah. Look how tiny the little feet are Mag.

MAGGIE: They'll have to go in the sale.

ALEC: Oh I know. But I thought you could have first knockings.

PEG: Ah, that's kind. To think of us.

MAGGIE: Yeah.

ALEC: That's me. All heart! Trouble is they're not handing out medals for redistributing a few baby clothes to a good home.

PEG: So you're in it for the glory are you?

ALEC: Nothing but.

PEG: They're lovely. Thank you.

ALEC: Have you heard anything from Rob?

MAGGIE: No. Not yet.

ALEC: He's a good bloke. Good company. Knows how to tell a story.

MAGGIE: Tell me.

ALEC: Well there was this man, had a dog and a pig…

MAGGIE and ALEC laugh. PEG's going through the bag of donated knitwear and holds up a knitted bathing suit.

PEG: Oh my God. You remember these?

MAGGIE: I remember yours.

PEG: My nan knitted it specially for me.

MAGGIE: Red and white stripes. It were lovely.

PEG: Very respectable. Up to the neck.

MAGGIE: You thought you were the bees knees in that bathing suit.

PEG: Till I got in the water and the weight of it damn near drowned me. And then it stretched. Came out with the straps down here and the crotch sunk to around my knees, practically topless and looking like I'd done some'at in my pants.

ALEC: Fetching image.

PEG: I can tell you this – put me off knitting for life.

MAGGIE: Have you seen Leonore? She hasn't been down to the centre for days now.

PEG: I'd just like to make it clear that was nothing to do with me.

ALEC: Of course not. Why would you…

PEG: I've nothing against her personally. I just can't take to Germans. Not at the moment.

MAGGIE: She's not Germans, she's Leonore.

PEG: Oh and I suppose those Jerry soldiers aiming their anti-aircraft guns up at our planes are saying "Hang on. That's Peg's brother Rob, hold your fire, he's a good un, we'll not shoot him down in flames".

MAGGIE: Don't take on…

PEG: No chance. They're going "enemy plane, die you English bastards".

MAGGIE: Nobody thinks it was you.

PEG: I'm not a bad person.

MAGGIE: D'you want a brew?

PEG starts to cry.

PEG: No. I want all these strangers who've invaded us gone. I want Alf. And a new coat that fits me, and us going out for a drive to Conniston of a Sunday and Alf getting us lost on the way back and the street lights and windows in the valley guiding us home. Not dark everywhere you look.

MAGGIE: It'll be over soon.

PEG: Will it?

ALEC: You could do with a good night's sleep. Are you getting your extra milk?

PEG: Yeah, and orange juice.

ALEC: Glass of hot milk before you go to bed then. Come on, I'll see you home.

PEG: It's only next door.

ALEC: And it's snowing again. Take my arm. Don't want you slipping over. Not when you're carrying tomorrow.

MAGGIE: Night love. Bless you.

GRAN starts to sing "Bless 'Em All"

ALEC: Night Maggie.

ALEC and PEG exit. GRAN extricates herself from the wool and heads upstairs.

MAGGIE: You off up, Gran?

GRAN waves yes and exits still singing.

Call me if you need a hand.

MAGGIE sits at the table and winds up the mess of wool GRAN's left behind. HILDA moves closer to her.

How's the throat?

They both know she made this up.

MAGGIE: When I shouted at you the other day. It wasn't your fault.

HILDA moves closer.

Unlike Leonore's knitting. Which was.

HILDA waits.

I'm sorry.

Beat. HILDA gently touches the bruise on MAGGIE's face.

I'm not hurt. It was an accident.

HILDA: I didn't mean to. I were just…

MAGGIE: Angry. I know.

HILDA: When he came home I didn't think he was very nice.

MAGGIE: Rob? He's a good kind man. Things take a bit of getting used to. Remember when you first came here, you wouldn't speak to anyone, even Tinker ran away from you? Now your bed's his favourite spot. Calls it home.

HILDA smiles.

HILDA: Cats don't speak.

MAGGIE: They purr. I tried to change your sheets the other day and he swore at me.

HILDA: Cats don't swear.

MAGGIE: They do too.

HILDA: How?

MAGGIE impersonates a swearing cat. HILDA laughs and copies her.

HILDA: That's how cats say, I wish you'd just bugger off and die.

MAGGIE: Where d'you hear that? Hilda? It's all right, you can tell me. I won't be cross.

In the street?

Beat.

At home?

Beat.

HILDA: *(Quietly)* "If it wasn't for you I wouldn't be trapped here."

MAGGIE holds her breath.

HILDA: "I wish you'd never been born."

MAGGIE: Oh Hilda. Poor baby. That won't happen again. You can stop home with us.

HILDA: He doesn't want me here.

MAGGIE: I'll sort it out. You can stay as long as you like.

MAGGIE holds HILDA close, then starts to hum to her, HILDA joins in happily "You Are My Sunshine".

End of scene.

Scene change song: "You Are My Sunshine"

SCENE FOUR

Kitchen.

Kitchen. Four days later. Monday early evening. PERCE, MAGGIE, HILDA, and GRAN are replete after their tea. MAGGIE is taking down strips of torn sheet dyed red or blue which have been hanging over the stove to dry, to create a union jack banner.

MAGGIE: You did say you wanted a big Union Jack didn't you Hilda?

HILDA: It's for the concert, Aunty Maggie. Bigger the better Miss said.

MAGGIE: Clearly Miss wasn't making it.

PERCE: That were a pie to remember Maggie. Thanks.

MAGGIE: No. Thanks to you for the pigeons.

JEAN enters in dressing gown and hair wound up in a towel.

JEAN: Oh sorry. If I'd known you were still here Perce I'd have stayed dressed.

PERCE whimpers unable to speak. JEAN sits next to him at the table and starts to do her nails.

MAGGIE: Not out this evening?

JEAN: Beauty night. Owe it to the troops. Got to keep up morale.

PERCE: Forward to Victory. Back up the Fighting Forces.

JEAN: That sort of thing. That was delicious pastry.

PERCE: Where did you get the fat?

MAGGIE: *(Avoiding the question.)* Hilda's a dab hand at pastry now aren't you love?

HILDA: I crimped the edges and I did the H on the top.

JEAN: Now let me see, H, what could that stand for? Holidays?

MAGGIE: Hah, what are those?

JEAN: Hogmanay?

MAGGIE: Bit early.

PERCE: Harvest?

MAGGIE: Bit late.

HILDA: It's an H for Hilda!

JEAN: Really?

GRAN: Hello.

MAGGIE: Yes Gran?

GRAN: Hello.

MAGGIE: We heard you the first time.

GRAN: HELLO!

JEAN: It's all right Mrs S, no need to shout.

PERCE: *(Catching on.)* Hi!

HILDA: Hey!

MAGGIE: Give me strength.

PERCE: Hi ho.

GRAN: *Singing. "Hi Ho Hi Ho As Off To Work We Go"*

   JEAN, PERCE and HILDA march round singing "Hi Ho"

MAGGIE: So how's things over at Thirlmere then Perce?

PERCE: Can't talk about it.

MAGGIE: Oh right. Top Secret.

PERCE: Tittle Tattle Lost the Battle.

MAGGIE: I heard the Germans had landed Thursday night.

PERCE: That were a mistake.

JEAN: Jolly would have been, old thing.

PERCE: It were very bright.

HILDA: Was it a bomb?

MAGGIE: It was nothing love, just the Northern Lights in the sky. Cept Perce and his mates mistook it for an invasion.

PERCE: Got to keep on our toes. Alert. Vigilant. Careless Talk Costs Lives.

MAGGIE: *(Clearing space on the table to lay the sheet on which the blue and red strips will be sewn.)* Come on you lot, give us a bit of space here.

Clearing away, JEAN picks up a nearly empty bottle of castor oil, sniffs it, tries a bit on her hand and rubs it in. It does the trick. She does the other hand and then pulls out a pair of white cotton gloves from her dressing gown pocket.

Here Gran. You hold the picture.

GRAN: Righty oh. Is it a game?

MAGGIE: No Gran it's a Union Jack. Or will be many stitches later. Jean what are you doing?

JEAN: You wouldn't believe the state of my hands. I could grate carrots on them. I pinched a bit of your castor oil Mrs S. You're getting pretty low. Hope you're not in need.

MAGGIE: I'll get you some more from the doctors.

GRAN: I don't take it. Horrible stuff, gives you the squitters.

HILDA giggles. PERCE joins in till he sees JEAN looking at him. He stops.

MAGGIE: Thank you Gran.

PERCE: I've got a new trick.

JEAN: For the concert party? Oh do show!

PERCE digs into his pocket.

It's not a creature with teeth is it?

PERCE: It's a rope.

JEAN: *(Relieved.)* Hurrah!

HILDA: *(Helping MAGGIE lay out the strips of fabric.)* Is it skipping?

PERCE: Er no.

HILDA: I can do skipping.

PERCE: It's not skipping. But I do need an assistant.

He looks straight at JEAN who is examining the state of her feet with dismay. PERCE coughs.

JEAN: Sorry?

HILDA: I'll be your assistant.

MAGGIE: Hilda, I need you here.

JEAN: Me?

PERCE: If you wouldn't mind.

JEAN: Do I have to wear spangley things?

PERCE: *(Imagination on fire.)* Won't be necessary. Thanks all the same. Now then…spangley.

MAGGIE: *(Prompting him.)* The trick, Perce?

PERCE: Oh aye. A rope. You see this rope. Take an ordinary rope.

GRAN: It's a piece of string.

PERCE: Slightly thicker. More like rope. Tie a knot in the ends, so.

(The rope is now a circle.)

And place it round the neck of my lovely assistant here.

JEAN: Beauty treatment's working then!

MAGGIE: Not tight, Perce.

PERCE: Ignore heckling. And abra cadabra, it's gone straight through her neck and it's at the back!

No one is more amazed that PERCE's sleight of hand has worked than he is. HILDA claps.

HILDA: Do it again.

MAGGIE: Well done Perce!

PERCE: And place it round the neck of my lovely assistant here… and abra cadabra!

He successfully repeats the trick.

HILDA: More, more!

PERCE: Right, ladies and gentlemen…

With a flourish PERCE drapes the length of rope over his wrist and then round, then turns to JEAN.

Drape the rope over and round and cross and and if my lovely lovely here would care to er…er… oh yes, to tie my wrists together now. That's it, tight as you like. Aaah, not quite so tight.

JEAN: Sorry maestro.

PERCE: Who?

JEAN: *(With a flourish, acting the part.)* And here he is ladies and gentlemen, bound at the wrists. Can he break free? Can he…

PERCE: *(Turning away.)* Er…er…tara!

To everyone's surprise he turns back and his hands are free.

MAGGIE: Perce you're a genius!

JEAN: Magic!

JEAN impulsively hugs PERCE who has a rush of bravado to the head.

PERCE: Don't Alight From A Moving Bus.

JEAN: *(Slightly bemused.)* I won't. What's next?

PERCE: The chair. You tie me to the chair.

GRAN: And beat him with sticks!

MAGGIE: Gran!

GRAN: That's what they did in the film.

HILDA: Can I help?

JEAN: Of course. You can be the lovely assistant's lovely assistant.

PERCE: Good strong knots. And the wrists, at the back.

PEG enters.

PEG: Oh hello am I missing a party?

MAGGIE: A rehearsal. Did you bring the pins?

PEG: There you go. *(Whispering.)* What was it like?

MAGGIE: Really tasty. I saved you a bit.

PEG: I don't think I better, not in my condition.

MAGGIE: Probably for the best.

JEAN: There!

GRAN: Now do we hit him with sticks?

MAGGIE: There's no hitting. It's magic.

GRAN: I liked the sticks.

PEG: I've not seen him do this one before.

PERCE does some wriggling but stays tied up.

JEAN: Did we do it too tight?

PERCE: *(Beginning to panic.)* It'll be fine. Fine.

PEG: We should try this on Sidney.

GRAN: Why's he gone all red in the face?

PEG: Probably the castor oil.

JEAN: What castor oil?

MAGGIE: Peg!

PEG: Sorry.

GRAN: Filthy stuff. Gives you the…

MAGGIE: It's safe. It's been cooked. You all enjoyed it.

JEAN: Pastry. You put in the pastry?

MAGGIE: Only a few tablespoons. You can't have pigeon pie without a crust and we've had our fat ration this week. We'll be fine.

JEAN: We'll be regular. That's for certain. You all right there Perce old thing?

Peg suddenly lets out a scream.

MAGGIE: What's the matter? Peg?

JEAN: Please tell me you're not in labour.

PEG: *(Climbing onto a chair.)* It ran across there.

JEAN: Jesus!

PEG: No, a mouse.

JEAN: Oh for…

MAGGIE: Jean! Child in the room!

HILDA: Here mouse, come on mouse.

PEG is now on the table. JEAN tries to join her.

JEAN: Move over.

PEG: *(Pushing her off.)* There's no room.

JEAN: There is too. Ow!

PEG: Anyway I'm pregnant.

JEAN: So?

MAGGIE: There it goes.

MAGGIE grabs a rolling pin. JEAN screams and leaps onto PERCE's lap, keeping her feet well above floor level.

HILDA: No, no don't hurt it.

PEG/JEAN: *(Together.)* Hurt it!

HILDA: Please Aunty Maggie.

MAGGIE: All right. All right. Don't scare it.

PEG: Scare it?! What about me?

MAGGIE: Quiet everyone. Hilda get the bucket.

JEAN clings tighter to PERCE who looks like he's about to have a heart attack and die happy. HILDA and MAGGIE stalk the mouse with the bucket.

Gently. It's in the corner. Just there. Yes!

The mouse is trapped under the bucket.

JEAN: You're absolutely sure it's under there?

MAGGIE: You're safe now. Though I think Perce could do with a cup of cold water. Maybe this trick needs a bit more work.

MAGGIE unties him.

GRAN: I told you. Should have used the sticks.

PEG: You're not leaving it in there all night are you?

MAGGIE: We'll let it free in the garden.

HILDA: Can't I keep it? Please please can't I keep it?

MAGGIE: Wouldn't be fair. Tinker would eat it for breakfast.

JEAN: Three cheers for Tinker!

MAGGIE: Anyway it's got its own home somewhere else.

JEAN: We fervently hope.

MAGGIE: It's a field mouse.

JEAN: Long as it's gone by the time I come down to breakfast.

PEG: Perce give us a hand down.

JEAN: Though if your pie works, might all be down sooner. Night Perce. Don't worry, practice makes perfect, keep at it, as the actress said to the bishop.

PERCE is looking shell shocked.

PEG: Perce! Home.

PEG and PERCE leave. JEAN exits to bed.

MAGGIE: You get off upstairs Hilda love. I'll be up in a minute, tuck you in, when I've tidied round a bit.

HILDA: If we can't keep the mouse…

MAGGIE: Yes?

HILDA: I've never had a pet.

MAGGIE: We've got Tinker.

HILDA: He's old.

MAGGIE: *(Pulling her onto her knee.)* Tell you what. Maisie Hibbert's kittens are due to leave their mother soon. If they're healthy, how about you chose one of them?

HILDA: Like you chose me, at the Pavilion?

MAGGIE: And just as cuddly.

Planting a kiss on HILDA's cheek, MAGGIE tips her off.

Off to bed now, sweetheart. Night night.

HILDA: Sleep tight. Mind the bugs don't bite.

MAGGIE: If they do

HILDA: Just squeeze them tight and they won't bite another night.

HILDA goes off happily chanting. MAGGIE starts to shuffle a baking tray under the bucket. There's a knock at the door. MAGGIE's hands are full.

MAGGIE: Come in! What've you forgotten?

Knocking continues.

Gran go and let Peg in would you? She must have her hands full, like me.

GRAN goes off.

Come on then Mr Mouse.

HILDA: *(Off.)* Aunty Maggie!

MAGGIE: *(Smiling.)* I'll be up in a minute love. Snuggle down. Sweet dreams.

GRAN enters.

MAGGIE: What'd she leave behind?

GRAN: It's not Peg.

MAGGIE: Who then?

GRAN: It's someone from the RAF. For you.

End of scene.

Scene change song: "You Are My Sunshine"

SCENE FIVE

Hall. Three days later, Thursday night.

A few days later. Night.

MAGGIE is finishing clearing up, putting her coat on, turning the lights off when ALEC enters.

ALEC: Hello?

MAGGIE: Oh, you frightened me!

ALEC: I'm sorry.

MAGGIE: No, it's me. I'm jumpy.

ALEC: In what way?

MAGGIE: No no I'm fine. It's nothing medical. Everyone's gone. I was just closing up. Did you want something?

ALEC: I only heard today. About Hilda.

MAGGIE: Ah. The Keswick grapevine.

ALEC: Yes.

MAGGIE: It'll be in the Reminder next week.

ALEC: If it isn't in the Reminder it hasn't..?

MAGGIE: Yes well it has. She's gone home. And life goes on.

ALEC: What happened?

MAGGIE: You mean you haven't heard all the details?

ALEC: I'm not here to gossip.

MAGGIE: I'm sorry. Like I said, I'm jumpy.

ALEC: People are concerned about you.

MAGGIE: Why? Am I not functioning? Seems to me I've done my share down here. See anyone else staying this late?

ALEC: No. And you look exhausted.

MAGGIE: Thanks very much. You know how to make a girl feel good about herself.

ALEC: Not a girl. A woman who's lost a child.

MAGGIE: Oh I think you're exaggerating a bit there. For a start, she's not dead and for an end, she's not my child. Never was, never will be.

ALEC: They leave their mark though don't they, kids, on a house?

MAGGIE: Yes. I hate going home nights. Still, I've got Gran. She's only one step off from childhood herself. Mind, she gave Hilda's dad a very adult earful when she realised what he'd come for.

ALEC: You had no warning?

MAGGIE: No. I was in my kitchen dying sheets to make Union Jack for the concert. Next thing I know there's a knock at the door and there's a strange man in RAF uniform asking for me. I thought something had happened to Rob. My guts turned to water. Then he said he was Hilda's dad and I was so relieved I had to rush to the lavvy. Sorry.

ALEC: It's often how the body responds to shock. You're not alone.

MAGGIE: Just thinking of it…

ALEC: Sit yourself down…that's it.

MAGGIE sits. ALEC beside her as she recovers herself.

MAGGIE: I'm sorry to be so foolish.

ALEC: It's all right Maggie.

MAGGIE: I keep telling myself she's not dead, he's her father, he's got every right, but the way she stood there with her little suitcase and her face all peaky and tense like she gets when she's trying not to cry. It just breaks my heart.

ALEC: Her mum must be very grateful to you for taking care of her all these months.

MAGGIE: No, if that were it I could…I don't know, it'd be easier maybe…but she doesn't want her back, she wrote asking me to take Hilda on…

ALEC: Adopt her?

MAGGIE: Yeah. But then her dad found out and come hot foot to claim her.

ALEC: She's wanted then.

MAGGIE: Yes. Of course she is…who wouldn't want Hilda?…

ALEC: *(Prompting.)* But?

MAGGIE: This is a terrible thing to say…

ALEC: I won't tell a soul.

MAGGIE: I don't know if he really does, want her. I mean, how's he going to take care of her?

ALEC: Her mum…

MAGGIE: No, she's…they're not together…

ALEC: Grandparents maybe?

MAGGIE: She's never mentioned them. I said I'd look after her till the war was over and he came back but he wouldn't have it. He was just so cold, you know, like angry behind his eyes. I felt like a thief. But Hilda was pleased to see him. And I'm sure it'll be all right, you know, like you say, there'll be aunties and uncles or grandparents. Her family, flesh and blood. I'm sure it'll all be all right in the end.

MAGGIE breaks down.

Except it isn't. It isn't all right. Nothing is.

MAGGIE rubs her chest, crying.

MAGGIE: It hurts. Real pain, here. Oh I'm just being stupid. I know. Stupid stupid woman. I'm sorry. There's folks far worse off. What must you think of me?

ALEC: I think you're doing fine.

MAGGIE: Really?

ALEC: Really.

MAGGIE: *(Blowing her nose.)* That's your professional opinion is it?

ALEC: Absolutely.

MAGGIE: I must look a sight.

ALEC: You look fine.

MAGGIE: Is that your professional opinion too?

He looks away.

MAGGIE: Sorry. Sorry.

ALEC: Blaming yourself again?

He takes her hands in his.

You are a remarkable woman Maggie. You make a home for anyone who needs it. You run this place. And all the time you take care of everyone.

MAGGIE: *Looking down at his hand shaking her head.*

No.

ALEC: You have to let your friends take care of you sometimes.

MAGGIE notices his signet ring.

MAGGIE: Who's RJC?

ALEC: Sorry?

MAGGIE: On your ring?

ALEC: Oh. My brother.

MAGGIE: I thought you just had sisters.

ALEC: And a brother.

MAGGIE: Oh.

ALEC: He died.

MAGGIE: I'm sorry. In the war?

ALEC: No.

MAGGIE: Folks don't like to think bad things happened before all this kicked off do they? But they did. Childhood, best days of your life. I hope not. How old was he?

ALEC: He'd just finished his third year at med school. Brilliant student, headed for a first, everyone loved him, especially women…

MAGGIE: He sounds a right pain.

ALEC: *(Laughing with surprise.)* How'd you know that? And you an only child?

MAGGIE: I've lived alongside Peg the Competitor all my life. One day I'll get my head round the fact I can't win. Get used to coming second.

ALEC: You never get used to that.

MAGGIE: No?

ALEC: Put it this way, I wasn't in his league.

MAGGIE: How did it happen?

ALEC: Motorbike. Village outside Glasgow. Wet road, late at night. My father identified him by his ring. Dad retired soon after that. Gave up. They both did.

MAGGIE: What about your sisters?

ALEC: Oh they'd gone by then. Married.

MAGGIE: Leaving you.

ALEC: Leaving me.

MAGGIE: It's a nice ring.

ALEC: Maggie.

MAGGIE: I've never talked to anyone like this before, you know,…I mean, I left school at 14. I'm just an ordinary person.

ALEC: No you're not. You're…luminous.

MAGGIE: Luminous?

ALEC: It means…

MAGGIE: I know what it means. Full of light.

ALEC: Full of light.

MAGGIE: Full of shit. I'm a married woman!

ALEC: *(Unrepentant.)* Doesn't stop you being luminous.

MAGGIE: And doesn't make me daft either. What're you playing at?

ALEC: I'm sorry. But you're just wonderful. You're true.

MAGGIE: Am I heck!

ALEC: And you don't know it. A truly wonderful woman.

MAGGIE: Have you been drinking?

Beat.

ALEC: Yes probably I have. I apologise. Will you forgive me?

MAGGIE: For what? You've not done anything, have you?

ALEC: Except call you luminous.

MAGGIE: Not a hanging crime yet, far as I'm aware. Not in this country anyroad.

ALEC: Can I give you a lift home?

MAGGIE: I can walk thank you.

ALEC: Course you can. You can do anything you want.

MAGGIE: *(Rueful.)* Oh yeah?

ALEC: It's a free country isn't it?

MAGGIE: You really don't come from round here do you?

ALEC: Sadly, no. I wish…

MAGGIE: What?

ALEC: I wish I were different. Goodnight.

He turns to leave.

MAGGIE: Alec?

She goes to him. They kiss passionately, stop, she moves away slightly.

Goodnight.

ALEC leaves.

End of scene.

Scene change song: "Love Is The Sweetest Thing"

SCENE SIX

Nine days later. Saturday evening.

PEG is making up her face/getting ready with help from JEAN. GRAN is in a chair, dozing. LEONORE is watching in the wings, waiting to go on.

PEG: How long've we got?

JEAN: *(Consulting a list pinned to the wall.)* Two more to go then Alec doing his Kipling recitation, then you and Maggie.

PEG: I think I'm going to be sick.

JEAN: No you're not.

PEG: Maggie's been in the toilet a long time. D'you think she's okay?

JEAN: She'll be fine. You'll be fine.

PEG: We've only been through it once just the two of us. And that was only the moves. She wouldn't sing it without...you know, Hilda.

JEAN: You'll be fine.

PEG: You're beginning to get on my nerves.

JEAN: There, you look lovely.

PEG: *(Jumping up and practicing her steps.)* Nobody's fine. Least of all Maggie. How could she be? I'd have told him where he could get off. Marching in like that. Sweeping the child off. Why didn't anyone stop him?

JEAN: I was tucked up in bed in my pj's.

PEG gives her a look.

I know, novel experience, but hey a girl's got to get some sleep sometime. I thought it was Rob come home unexpectedly so I stayed put. Came down next morning and she'd gone.

PEG: He can't do that!

JEAN: He's the girl's father. I suppose he can do what he likes.

PEG: I wish Sidney's father'd come and whisk him off home.

JEAN: Threaten to adopt him and he might.

PEG: I couldn't take the risk. I wish she'd just say something. We've always talked about everything but since Hilda's been gone, she's sort of closed off. It's like Hilda never existed.

JEAN: I know Maggie was fond of her, but she was just a child and somebody elses's at that. I mean if staff got like that at boarding schools, falling for the children and wanting to keep them, it'd be utter chaos. Though come to think of it, it might have been quite nice. It'd have kept my buttocks away from the dreadful Pinkie and his oversized teeth.

PEG: I wouldn't say anything to Maggie. Pinkie or not.

JEAN: OK you're the boss. How's Rex?

PEG: Still limping, poor dog. I don't know why Perce couldn't have sawn Sidney in half.

JEAN: So what's he doing now, instead of magic?

PEG: Secret. God help us.

JEAN: The hem's a bit longer on this side than the other.

PEG fiddles with the waistband.

PEG: Oh right.

JEAN: Up a bit. Stop. Down a bit. No, up again. Nearly…

PEG: It's a Keswick concert, not the bloody Ritz. If it droops a bit on one side it'll be just like the rest of us.

JEAN: Speak for yourself.

PEG: I am. Have you not noticed what's happened to my chest?

JEAN: Hard to miss. You could sell tickets.

PEG: When Alf had those two days on leave he was like a dog with two tails. I kept telling him, they're not toys.

JEAN: Are they uncomfortable?

PEG: In too small underwear they are. If somebody doesn't donate a giant bra to the war effort soon I'm going to have to fix up something with ropes and pulleys.

She lowers her voice.

Perce came across some parachute silk. I'd be prepared to negotiate if you hear of anything elastic that's got a bit of life in it. Oh Maggie there you are! You're cutting it fine. All right?

MAGGIE enters.

MAGGIE: Fine.

PEG exchanges a significant look with JEAN.

PEG: Really?

MAGGIE: Where's Leonore?

PEG nods towards the wings.

PEG: Watching.

MAGGIE: It sounds ever so quiet out there.

PEG: It's Loudey Pete doing something with handkerchiefs and a ferret. They're probably all in shock.

MAGGIE: How many people are there in the audience? No don't tell me…

JEAN: Lorna says they'd sold nearly a hundred tickets by the end of last week.

MAGGIE: Oh god.

PEG: Jean, you're not helping. Distract us. Talk about your sex life or something like you normally do. You want to just walk through the dance with me Mag?

MAGGIE: We know it backwards.

PEG: Then let's do it forwards.

They mark through the stroll routine, squares, step ball change etc. very efficiently. LEONORE approaches.

JEAN: Well he's 6 foot two, with the most adorable little dimple.

MAGGIE: Lorna said she wanted the running order.

LEONORE: It's here.

JEAN: Don't you want to know where?

PEG: Not really.

MAGGIE: She sailed out front to tête a tête in the interval.

PEG: Let's just quickly go through the song. Please?

MAGGIE: Must we?

JEAN: I'll be the audience.

PEG: Leonore, count us in.

LEONORE: Two three and…

PEG pulls MAGGIE into the centre of the room.

PEG/MAGGIE: (*Singing together.*)

Everybody do the blackout stroll

Roundabout the town we'll all but go

We can live as happily as Old King Cole

MAGGIE can't go on.

PEG, SOLO: (*Singing.*) Once you get together in the Blackout Stroll.

PEG: Maggie? Oh love.

MAGGIE: I can't do this.

JEAN: It'll be fine.

PEG: Jean, shut up.

GRAN: (*Singing.*) There's no more cuddling in the moonlight
There's no more petting in the park
But smile, less worry over moonlight
For when we're strolling in the park,
It's lovely!

Everyone is astonished. JEAN starts to applaud.

JEAN: Bravo Mrs S!

PEG: Do you know all of it?

GRAN: I've heard it often enough.

PEG: Oh Maggie. We should.

MAGGIE: *(Blowing her nose.)* Absolutely not.

GRAN: *(Background.)*

> Everybody do the blackout stroll
> Roundabout the town we'll all but go
> We can live as happily as Old King Cole
> Once you get together in the Blackout Stroll.

PEG: Oh please. We've worked so hard.

MAGGIE: No.

PEG: This'll be great for her.

MAGGIE: Stuff her.

PEG: *(Giggling.)* I can't believe you just said that.

MAGGIE: Well I did. She may be able to sing but she sure as hell can't dance.

PEG: We'll dance round her.

GRAN: I'm not a maypole.

PERCE enters.

PERCE: Who's a maypole?

JEAN: Oh go on. You've got time to run through it. The doc's on before you.

PEG: I need some air. I'm all dizzy.

PEG exits. Off/onstage there's the sound of applause.

PERCE: Who's that?

JEAN goes and looks onstage.

JEAN: It appears to be a panto cow.

MAGGIE: That's the Thwaites. They're singing.

JEAN: They are too. I don't believe this. They're not. They are. Yes, it's Lilli Marlene.

Off we hear the strains of a rather muffled "Lilli Marlene".

GRAN: Sing with me Maggie. Go on. It'd be fun.

MAGGIE: Who for?

GRAN: Stella.

MAGGIE: Gran, Mum's dead. She's been dead for fifteen years.

GRAN: So?

MAGGIE: So when she was alive she paid more attention to her bloody piano than me! I'd not give her the satisfaction.

GRAN: For me then. Go on.

GRAN digs her in the ribs.

JEAN: Yes, go on.

MAGGIE: All right. On one condition. I'm never doing this again and you stay absolutely still.

JEAN: That's two.

MAGGIE: Shut up Jean.

JEAN: Certainly will.

MAGGIE: Gran? Okay, absolutely still?

GRAN: Only if I go to the lavvy first.

GRAN exits. From off/onstage there's a bang, screams and "Lilli Marlene" abruptly stops.

JEAN: What was that?

MAGGIE: Shots? Was that shots?

LEONORE: My God!

PERCE grabs a broom and rushes onstage in full home guard mode.

PERCE: Stand back. I'm coming through.

More shots and then a panto cow runs from the other side of the onstage through the backstage area and off again pursued by a small masked and hooded figure firing a cap gun. PERCE runs after them waving his broom.

PERCE: Where'd he go?

MAGGIE: Out there.

PERCE runs off.

JEAN: Who was that?

MAGGIE: Sidney. Who else?

JEAN: You don't know that for sure.

MAGGIE: I do. He was wearing Peg's front room curtains. Hold on, who's next? Where's Alec? Where's the doctor?

JEAN: I know who Alec is.

MAGGIE: I don't care who he is, where is he?

JEAN: I don't know. I've not seen him all evening.

MAGGIE: Leonore?

LEONORE: No.

MAGGIE: So it's one more act, then us. Go and find Peg. And don't tell her about the…

JEAN: Curtains?…What d'you take me for? Posh floosie with no brains? Don't worry, I won't.

JEAN exits.

MAGGIE: *(Calling off.)* Gran! Get off the lav, now! Maybe he's been delayed with a case.

LEONORE: Don't worry. Everyone out there is on your side.

MAGGIE: Oh Leonore. I'm glad you're playing for us. We couldn't do it without you.

LEONORE: Of course. It's what I do. Play the piano.

MAGGIE: And rescue people. *(Beat.)* Sorry. Have you heard… anything?

LEONORE: No. Not yet.

MAGGIE: I'm sorry.

LEONORE: It's not your fault.

MAGGIE: But the knitting was. Hilda…

LEONORE: Don't worry. I know.

MAGGIE: How did you know it was her?

LEONORE: War affects children in different ways. Have you heard…anything?

MAGGIE: No.

LEONORE: Not yet. As you say, "No news is…

MAGGIE: Is agony.

LEONORE: Yes, my dear. It is. *(Beat.)* For us all. We share this.

There's the sound off/on stage of "Vilia Oh Vilia" sung by a very wobbly contralto. JEAN and GRAN and PEG enter.

MAGGIE: Gran where've you been? You need a costume.

PEG: You'll never guess what!

MAGGIE: Oh no. You've seen Sidney.

PEG: No. Why?

MAGGIE: No reason.

JEAN: Wait till you hear this Maggie.

PEG: I'm telling her.

MAGGIE: It can wait. First find Gran a costume.

JEAN looks around for costume ideas, spots a box of dressing up clothes and finds something inappropriate like a feather headdress and pearls to put on GRAN.

JEAN: This do?

MAGGIE: Here Gran get these on, we're on stage next. Alec's not shown up.

PEG: I know. And I've just been told why.

JEAN and MAGGIE help GRAN into her bizarre outfit. JEAN gives her some red lipstick and eyebrow pencil.

JEAN: You'll never believe this…

PEG gives her a look.

All right. All right.

MAGGIE: I hope he's okay.

PEG: He's done a bunk.

MAGGIE: No. He wasn't that nervous. He was reading the poem. Didn't even have to learn it.

JEAN: Wouldn't need to…where he was going.

MAGGIE: I hope he hasn't had a breakdown. His motor has been acting up lately.

PEG: Acting, oh yes. Indeed. He'd know all about acting.

MAGGIE: What are you talking about?

JEAN: His motor's fine.

PEG: It was last seen heading south towards Windermere.

MAGGIE: He must have been called out to a patient.

JEAN: He doesn't have patients! Not real ones.

PEG: Jean enough, I've warned you. Maggie, listen to me! He's legged it cos he's been found out. He's not a doctor!

MAGGIE: What?

JEAN: He's not a medico.

PEG: He's a fraud.

JEAN: Not a medical qualification to his name. So they say.

PEG: They? I told you that.

JEAN: Must be true then.

MAGGIE: No. There must have been a mistake.

PEG: Mistake my arse. The police are after him.

MAGGIE: Police? What for?

JEAN: Impersonation? Fraud? Imbezzlement? Chap's got a full house.

MAGGIE: There must be some mistake. He would never…

PEG: No, Dolly Lattimer told me there's a police notice outside the surgery, asking for information regarding the man passing himself off as Doctor Alec Cornish.

JEAN: They'll be asking all of us what we knew about him.

MAGGIE: How do'you mean?

PEG: Well, where he might have gone I suppose.

JEAN: They tracked my Uncle Rufus all over the country. Granny had to send him to Canada in the end poor old sausage. It was that or clink.

PEG: Your uncle was a con man?

JEAN: Oh yes. Probably still is. Charming chap, take your last sixpence and leave you with a warm glow. Granny adored him. Everyone did. Not unlike our dear doctor.

PEG: Oh my god!

MAGGIE: What?

PEG: He saw my bits. He wasn't a doctor and he saw my private oh my god!

PERCE appears breathless.

PERCE: Couldn't catch him.

PEG: Catch who?

JEAN: No one. A cow.

PERCE: Last seen gaan into George for a stiff whisky.

PERCE exits.

PEG: I'm sorry?

GRAN is looking at herself in a mirror.

JEAN: Cripes girls! Applause. You ready? Stand by. It's your number after this one. You look dandy Mrs S.

GRAN: No I don't. I look like a shit-arsed monkey.

GRAN, leaving JEAN open mouthed, heads off towards the wings. JEAN checks out MAGGIE and PEG's hair, outfits etc.

MAGGIE: I can't take this in. Alec wasn't…

PEG: A doctor. No. Sorry Maggie. Probably not even Alec.

MAGGIE: But who is he then?

PEG: God knows.

JEAN: I feel rather stupid.

PEG: Think feet in stirrups and imagine how stupid I feel.

JEAN: That's not good. Bastard.

MAGGIE: Alec's not a doctor. But…he treated people.

PEG: I know!

MAGGIE: He gave Gran medicine. He cured people.

JEAN: He must have had some training, just not qualified for some reason maybe?

PEG: Like what?

JEAN: I don't know. Maybe he ran out of money.

PEG: You can't be a half-doctor. You either are or you aren't. And he wasn't.

MAGGIE: I talked to him…

PEG: We all talked to him.

MAGGIE: Told him…things…

PEG: Me too. About constipation and oh my God wind…

JEAN: Do you think you could stop there?

PEG: If I could stop I'd not have gone to the doctor, would I?

MAGGIE: So he was lying all the time, about everything?

JEAN: Who knows?

PEG: Where's Gran gone?

JEAN: Oh bloody hell.

PEG and JEAN go off searching for GRAN.

MAGGIE: Did you know? About Alec?

LEONORE: How could I?

MAGGIE: He used to spend a lot of time at Lorna's.

LEONORE: A conspiracy?

MAGGIE: Sorry. Sorry. I didn't mean that. I feel like – I don't know. It's betrayal.

LEONORE: Yes.

MAGGIE: No, I mean me. I've betrayed…everyone, by trusting him…talking to him. He told me I could do…oh never mind. All lies.

LEONORE: Whatever he is not, Alec is a good man. When I had despair, he was very kind to me. He understands people.

MAGGIE: How to con them you mean.

LEONORE: Their feelings. He helped me talk about my family. Don't be ashamed of loving him.

MAGGIE: But I…I don't. Didn't. Not in that way. I'm married. No.

LEONORE: What then, if not love?

MAGGIE: He made me feel…capable of things.

LEONORE: Look around you Maggie. You are.

MAGGIE: I'm all confused. I'm not saying it right. But it's like I'd talk to him and I'd feel…I don't know, better.

LEONORE: Isn't that what good doctors do?

MAGGIE: But he's not a doctor. He's a sham!

LEONORE: But all this? This place, this taking in of strangers, this working together against evil, for believe me Maggie it is evil what they are doing, this is not sham.

MAGGIE: No. I'm sorry.

GRAN enters.

LEONORE: Don't be sorry. What we have here, this is hope.

JEAN and PEG enter.

JEAN: Peg, you stay with her.

JEAN beckons LEONORE and MAGGIE to join PEG and GRAN who are herded into the wings.

JEAN: Leonore, Maggie? You're on girls.

PEG: I think I'm going to be sick.

JEAN: You'll be fine.

PEG turns on her. JEAN smiles sweetly.

JEAN: Trust me. I'm a toff.

LEONORE: *(To MAGGIE as she makes her way to the piano on stage.)* Knock them dead, ja?

PERCE enters and takes stuff out of the costume trunk.

JEAN: Oh, are these yours?

PERCE: It's a surprise.

JEAN looks at the small fairy outfit he's holding.

JEAN: Well it certainly will be.

PERCE: For you.

JEAN: For anyone I'd say. I didn't know you were into dressing up. I thought it was just magic, making people disappear and all that sort of jolly thing.

PERCE: I don't do magic any more.

JEAN: That's a shame. I was rather looking forward to being sawn in half.

PERCE: I couldn't hurt you. Not even in a magic way. And I don't want to make you disappear.

JEAN: Oh. Dear darling Perce. I'm not the one for you, you sweet old thing. But someone is. Someone out there is just dying to love you, whatever you dress up as, or make disappear. You've just got to keep your eyes peeled for her and forget all about me. In a few years' time I'm going to be a savage old harpy with two ex husbands soaked in gin and you won't even recognise me. I'll just be someone you once met during the war. This is the finale I'm afraid.

JEAN leans across and kisses PERCE deeply on the lips.

Goodbye Perce. You are now officially over me.

LEONORE on stage plays the intro music to "Blackout Stroll". JEAN moves to the wings to shepherd the trio on stage.

JEAN: Maggie first, then you Mrs S, then Peg.

MAGGIE: *(As they go "onstage".)* Now Gran remember. You don't move.

GRAN stops. PEG bangs into the back of her.

PEG: *(Shoving her.)* Not now. Once we get on stage.

GRAN: *(Crossly.)* No pushing!

They are all three onstage now, GRAN in the middle in her outrageous costume.

MAGGIE: *(Through a rictus smile.)* Okay okay you two. Smile.

Good evening ladies and gentlemen. We are…

To PEG and GRAN.

Who are we?

PEG: The Three Margarets.

MAGGIE smiles gratefully, then gestures to LEONORE to start the intro. GRAN copies the gesture. MAGGIE glares at her, pulling her hand back by her side. GRAN mouths "sorry".

MAGGIE: *(Out the corner of her mouth.)* Don't move.

GRAN stays rigidly still, grinning as they sing "Blackout Stroll" beautifully, MAGGIE and PEG dancing round her. When they get to the music only part GRAN can't restrain herself and starts to join in the dancing to great comedic effect. It looks like disaster's about to ruin everything but PEG and MAGGIE mutter to each other over GRAN's head.

Grab her.

They secure one of GRAN's arms each and manage the rest of the routine perfectly with GRAN suspended between them, feet not touching the floor, her feathered headdress hanging jauntily over one eye. At the end they walk off in perfect harmony, GRAN getting it right at last. They come back on for a bow and applause. As MAGGIE and PEG leave the stage GRAN stays there basking in the applause. They come back and get her off, smiling and waving and blowing kisses at her public.

In the wings they hug each other with glee.

JEAN: You were wonderful! Well done Mrs S! A triumph!

LEONORE fills with accompaniment to "It's A Lovely Day Tomorrow" onstage.

PEG: They liked us!

MAGGIE: We got away with it!

PEG: I wish we could do an encore.

MAGGIE: You must be insane. That was one of the scariest things I've ever done.

PEG: And how. But fun.

MAGGIE: Thank god you were there. I could never have managed that on my own in a million years.

A small gang of evacuees run past backstage.

PEG: What the hell are that lot doing here? Oi!

The evacuees are followed by PERCE.

MAGGIE: What's going on?

PERCE: It's a surprise.

MAGGIE: Certainly is. And not a good one.

PERCE: *(To JEAN.)* Wish me luck again?

JEAN: Better not. I think you need all your wits about you.

PERCE: Oh. Right. Your Country Needs You!

He hurries after the kids.

PEG: Please tell me he's not got them doing bird noises?

JEAN: I've no idea. Maybe he'll make them disappear.

PEG looks at MAGGIE. JEAN realises her mistake.

JEAN: Sorry. I didn't mean…put my foot in my mouth again, haven't I?

PEG: No love, more like your leg down your throat. You okay Mag?

MAGGIE nods. PERCE enters onstage and stands like a rabbit in the headlights.

Oh heck, look. He doesn't know what he's going to say next.

LEONORE does the intro music to "It's A Lovely Day Tomorrow"

PERCE looks desperately to the wings.

PEG: Somebody help him. Get him off.

MAGGIE: *(Under her breath.)* Come on Perce. You can do it.

PERCE: I'd… I'd…

PERCE looks desperately around for help. It comes from an unexpected quarter.

LEONORE: Ladies and gentlemen, I'd like to introduce Perce Howells and the Evacuees Choir.

PEG AND MAGGIE: Choir?!

JEAN: Sssh.

PERCE beckons into the other wings and the four evacuees enter. They are a motley crew dressed in an assortment of too small or too large dressing-up clothes.

LEONORE: Many of our children have coughs and colds and are not well enough to be here. So please welcome the children who have made it through the snow to sing to us tonight.

LEONORE starts to play the intro to "It's A Lovely Day Tomorrow" again.

PERCE sings with the children.

JEAN: Aah. Little angels.

PEG gives her a look.

PEG: You'll notice Sidney has not joined the heavenly choir.

JEAN: Yes he has.

PEG: Where?

JEAN: Well someone else has. Look there's one arrived late.

PEG: Oh my god. Maggie look...

MAGGIE turns from tending to GRAN to look and there, being beckoned onto the stage by PERCE to join the other evacuees is HILDA in snowcovered coat and boots. She joins in the singing, looking over to find MAGGIE. They finish the song. MAGGIE goes to the edge of the stage as the kids take their bow. HILDA comes to her.

MAGGIE: What are you doing here? What's happened?

HILDA: I ran away.

MAGGIE: Are you all right?

HILDA: I wanted to come home.

LEONORE launches into a final encore. HILDA pulls MAGGIE on stage to sing. She in turn beckons on PEG, GRAN and JEAN who all sing the finale, hopefully with the audience.

ALEC and ROB join the rest of the cast singing.

"It's A Lovely Day Tomorrow"

The End.